The Global Journalist

The Global Journalist

News and Conscience in a World of Conflict

Philip Seib

ROWMAN & LITTLEFIELD PUBLISHERS, INC.
Lanham • Boulder • New York • Toronto • Plymouth, UK

ROWMAN & LITTLEFIELD PUBLISHERS, INC.

Published in the United States of America
by Rowman & Littlefield Publishers, Inc.
A wholly owned subsidiary of The Rowman & Littlefield Publishing Group, Inc.
4501 Forbes Boulevard, Suite 200, Lanham, Maryland 20706
www.rowmanlittlefield.com

Estover Road
Plymouth PL6 7PY
United Kingdom

British Library Cataloguing-in-Publication Information Available

Library of Congress Cataloging-in-Publication Data Available

ISBN 0-7425-1101-4 (cloth : alk. paper)
ISBN 0-7425-1102-2 (pbk. : alk. paper)

Printed in the United States of America

♾™ The paper used in this publication meets the minimum requirements of
American National Standard for Information Sciences–Permanence of Paper for
Printed Library Materials, ANSI/NISO Z39.48-1992.

For Christine

It is not because I cannot explain that you won't understand, it is because you won't understand that I cannot explain.

—Elie Wiesel (at the opening of the Holocaust Museum)

Contents

Preface

This book examines journalism as a moral enterprise by exploring the relationship between news and foreign policy. The linkage is complex, reflecting changes in media technologies and economics as well as shifts in the values that govern international relations.

With the end of the Cold War, the geopolitical truisms that shaped news judgments as well as government policy were open to revision. Policymakers and journalists alike had the opportunity to redefine priorities. Undertaking humanitarian intervention, for example, which had primarily been a function of protecting strategic interests, now has become more of an ethical issue, which moves it onto terrain that neither governments nor news media have fully explored.

In many American news organizations, international coverage is accorded minimal importance. The conventional wisdom within substantial parts of the news business seems to be that international reporting costs too much and does too little to win and keep an audience. It makes more sense, so this thinking goes, to give the audience what it wants. If people want "news you can use"—what to feed your cat and yourself, and other equally helpful items—give it to them.

That may be logical when contemplating corporate profits, but it does not meet standards of professional responsibility. The rest of the world *is* important, and it is part of the journalist's job to keep the public apprised of what is going on in faraway places.

In these matters, principles of national policy run parallel to those of journalism. As the most powerful nation, the United States has duties of leadership, which it should not shirk. The news media have commensurate duties to cover events that affect the interests of the American government and the American people. Defined broadly, those interests include economic matters, security concerns, humanitarian issues, and much in between. There are plenty of stories to be told. The growth of the oil industry in former Soviet republics, for instance, will affect Americans' energy costs and will also affect the stability of a volatile region. A war in central Africa may seem to have little to do with Americans' daily lives, but the conflict—particularly if it is depicted vividly by the news media—might have considerable impact on Americans' consciences. That may influence decisions ranging from charitable giving to voting.

Events in the 1990s frequently tested post-Cold War moral resolve. In the Balkans, Rwanda, and elsewhere, governments' ability to assist people in trouble was not always matched by a willingness to do so. Similarly, news organizations were sometimes slow to respond to stories that were of great urgency to the people directly involved but of little perceived importance to others.

The impact of news coverage continues to be debated. The "CNN effect" is the supposed ability of coverage to influence policymaking. There is little evidence that this actually happens to a significant degree. Certainly, news reports can call attention to events and sometimes capture the public's interest, but only the most chaotic policymaking process would actually be driven by news coverage. As policy develops, news stories may be influential, but rarely if ever are they truly determinative.

Also the subject of continuing debate is Americans' attitude about their nation's role in the world. When various opinion surveys are studied, it is apparent that Americans are neither isolationist nor interventionist, but rather fall somewhere in between. The best description of their outlook is "cautious."

Despite this caution, intervention sometimes is appropriate. News coverage of the humanitarian crisis in Somalia in 1992 helped reinforce the Bush administration's decision to provide humanitarian assistance backed up by a military presence. When news coverage depicted things going bad, it was a factor in the decision to extricate American forces. The more complex situation in the Balkans produced a different level of American involvement and a different kind of news coverage. Some journalists, outraged by the horrors they witnessed and by what they believed to be an inadequate response by the international community, reconsidered the sanctity of "objectivity." They determined that their role should extend beyond providing balanced presentation of all sides' positions and instead should make clear who are the victims and who are the aggressors. Even within journalism circles, this embrace of advocacy is controversial.

In the 1994 Rwandan war, the magnitude of evil challenged the news media's ability to convey the reality of what was happening. Only belatedly did the world acknowledge that genocide had occurred. This sluggish response is not unusual when the war or other crisis takes place in Africa. The Rwanda story is an example of how race can be a subtle presence in both policymaking and news coverage decisions. That is something governments and news organizations should address.

Events in Rwanda and the Balkans also presented some journalists with a difficult choice about the extent of their responsibilities as witnesses to horrific events. Is their duty only to report what they see and let others act upon that information? Or should they feel obligated to present their information in other forums, such as by testifying in war crimes trials?

Even after an uneasy peace was imposed in Bosnia, trouble in the Balkans did not end. In 1999, NATO launched its first war when it decided to stop the expulsion of Kosovar Albanians from their homes. In addition to the importance of this war in reshaping European security policy, it was a testing ground for the news media. This was the first "Web war," with the Internet serving as an important means of gathering and disseminating information. News organizations had to address not only technology-related issues, but also adapt traditional standards—such as corroboration of sources' information—to the demands of Web-based news. And, as in any war, journalists needed to resist efforts by governments to push news coverage in politically convenient directions.

As the new century began, news organizations had to decide how best to use the limited resources they devote to international coverage. Judging what is most newsworthy continues to be one of the most important and difficult tasks of the news business. The international AIDS crisis, environmental concerns, persistent wars, and the effects of globalization were among the issues that received coverage, some of it substantive, much of it skimpy.

Issues are important only as they affect people, and millions continue to be affected in terrible ways by war, disease, famine, and poverty.

Much of the international community takes only passing notice of these sad conditions, and suffering continues. Neglect is never benign.

As this book was about to go the printer in September 2001, the United States was attacked by terrorists and thousands of people died. The U.S. government's immediate response included a vow to wage war on the perpetrators and the nations that harbored them.

This would not be the kind of war that is discussed in parts of this book—the "virtual war" that relies on high-tech weaponry and gives highest priority to eliminating American military casualties. Secretary of Defense Donald Rumsfeld said: "People think of the wars that we have seen lately, the kind of antiseptic wars where a cruise missile is fired off, shown on television landing in some smoke, and so forth. That is not what this is about."

For political leaders, soldiers, and journalists alike, defining "war" is particularly difficult when the enemy is not a state. Terrorists are elusive as military targets and as subjects of news reports.

Nevertheless, as this twenty-first-century war proceeds, journalists will be covering it. In this, as in the coverage of other global events, news organizations have the responsibility to resist jingoistic impulses and to present a complex story with evenhanded precision. This is one more test for the global journalist.

In the years ahead, there will be many more conflicts and issues to cover. The job of the news media is not to try to solve all the world's problems, but to shake awake the world's conscience. Good journalism can do that. Encouraging journalists and others to think about this is the purpose of this book.

Acknowledgments

Special thanks goes to Candice Quinn, my research assistant, who was thorough and tireless in searching through mountains of material, and who offered many useful suggestions as this book was coming together. Brenda Hadenfeldt, my editor at Rowman & Littlefield, once again provided valuable advice and displayed great patience. *The Journal of Conflict Studies* and *Harvard International Review* published articles drawn from early stages of the book. As always, Christine Wicker supplied priceless encouragement and love.

CHAPTER ONE

Collision: Technology, Money, and Ethics

The horrible images have become familiar, so often do we see them on television screens or newspaper pages. Children maimed by war or shriveled by hunger. Fields of bodies, felled by weapons or disease. We see them and react with sadness, sometimes anger.

How should the public respond to the events and policies behind these horrors? Political leaders may say these are not matters of "national interest" and so are none of our concern. The news media sporadically provide bursts of information that tend to be so lacking in context that the public rarely understands why these horrible things are happening or how they might be stopped.

What should be done?

In much of the global village, war and famine resist all attempts to eradicate them. Prosperity and opportunity spread slowly and erratically. Disease and environmental decay take their massive toll. An accurate, comprehensive picture of all this, presented by the news media, would be strikingly ugly, but that ugliness might touch the conscience of those who could do something about it.

Most news organizations, however, cover such matters only fleetingly. They are wary not so much of ugliness—devastation captures the public's attention—but of the complexity behind it. News organizations tend to keep coverage of faraway places short and simple. The news, after all, is a product, and it wouldn't do to overtax the presumably limited attention span of its consumers.

If this journalism of convenience prevails, chances of improving life in much of the world will be slim. If, however, the news media reassert their traditional values—such as the long-standing mandate to comfort the afflicted and afflict the comfortable—perhaps journalism will help foster change.

Doing good is possible. News coverage can influence public opinion, which in turn can nudge the policymaking process. At the end of this chain—sometimes—is progress. The hungry might be fed, the sick might be treated, the besieged might be rescued. Reaching this end is one challenge facing today's global journalist.

Entering the New Century

The global village is still under construction, but it has assumed a definite look and lifestyle. As a virtual community, it is bound together electronically. This is partly due to the Internet, which may prove to be transforming in ways comparable to the broadcast media and, some would say, even the printing press. To see evidence of this new cohesion, hopscotch the world with a few clicks of the mouse. Send an e-mail from Omaha to Ouagadougou. Scan the day's news from Bombay or Brasilia. Watch the legislature of your state discuss tax policy or the parliament of a distant country debate war and peace. It's all there, as close as if it were just down the street in your village. Anyone with a computer and access to the Internet can skitter across the Web to seek or deliver information. The quantity of material is vast, and its quality is uneven. What the public will do with it is still unknown.

The latest news technologies offer unmatched breadth and speed. Delays in news delivery are increasingly rare; anything less than real-time coverage seems archaic. Reaction to news, whether from the public or policymakers, has similarly increased in velocity.

The speed at which news moves is a relative matter. In *Paul Revere's Ride*, David Hackett Fischer charts what was then the rapid spread of the news about the first shots of the American Revolution, fired at Lexington on the morning of April 19, 1775. Word reached as far as Providence, Rhode Island, that night. By the following night, news of the clash was received in New London, Connecticut. A report reached New York City late on the 23rd and Philadelphia on the 24th. A handbill carried by an express rider got to Annapolis, Maryland, on April 26 and the story reached Williamsburg, Virginia, on the 28th; Charleston, South Carolina, on May 9 (by sea); and settlements in western Pennsylvania the second week in May.[1]

Today, anyone in those same American cities can see Baghdad being bombed on live television. They can watch real-time briefings from the Pentagon telephone or read e-mail reports from Iraqis while they are under attack. Good and evil from around the world arrive instantly in America's living rooms. Those who deliver information and those who respond to it must adjust to new definitions of timeliness.

Even assuming that high-speed communication is a blessing, there must be an intellectual and moral foundation on which the new, always-in-touch virtual community is built. This is particularly important to journalists who face the danger that their profession will be so technology-driven that the reasons for doing journalism are forgotten. Whatever size village the journalist covers, she or he has a responsibility to find and deliver information that the public needs. Sometimes that mission conflicts with speed and limits profits. Journalists must try to reconcile the varied demands placed on all who work in the news business.

Beyond the concerns about the mechanics and economics of journalism is the fact that news can make a difference in people's lives. From that basic truth rises a moral mandate that journalists and news consumers should recognize.

Defining Journalistic Responsibility

There is no precise formula for establishing intellectual independence, but part of the task for news organizations is to rely less on governments' priorities and take a more proactive approach when evaluating events around the world. This entails not just being more knowledgeable but also having a more sophisticated appreciation of the responsibilities of journalism as profession and the ethical duties of journalists individually.

First is the basic duty to inform, and especially to inform a broad audience. Journalist James Hoge has noted that "elites in business, the professions, and government have ample news and information sources. It is the general public that is being short-changed by media that have yet to exhibit the combination of effort and talent to make news of the wider world interesting and relevant."[2] Along these lines, British journalist Ian Hargreaves asked, "Why should we choose to live in an isolationist 'dumbtopia' precisely at the moment when there is almost nothing which affects our daily lives, whether at the economic, social, or cultural level, which is not in some sense globally charged or driven?"[3] Part of this duty to inform is to report the truth—not mere surmise or propaganda, but facts that are verified and explained.

Second, decisions about what to report and what to withhold are important not only as they relate to stories' newsworthiness, but also in terms of the effects of such decisions. Diplomacy sometimes works best outside the glare of media coverage, and journalists may decide to give diplomats a chance, at least briefly, to work with minimal visibility. Similarly, journalists may withhold information about intelligence or military operations. News executives making these decisions weigh the public's *right* to know and *need* to know, and add to the equation the responsibilities of citizenship. This does not mean acceding to every government request for secrecy based on vaguely defined "national security" concerns, but it does mean recognizing the realities of national interest in a contentious world.

Third, tone of coverage is important. The line between aggressive reporting and biased reporting can easily be crossed. As with the decision to publish or withhold, journalists should not surrender their aggressiveness in gathering information, nor should they disregard the effects of their coverage. Also, if reporters are unfailingly cynical in their stories, the public may get a distorted view of events and good-faith efforts to resolve a crisis may be undermined. Skepticism is often merited, such as when government action does not match government pronouncements, but when that skepticism leads to an unshakable presumption of incompetence or malfeasance, it may have gone too far.

Fourth, journalists should recognize that their coverage may affect opinion and policy. News organizations exercise considerable power when they decide to go to or stay away from a distant trouble spot. Where cameras go, attention and aid are much more likely to follow. That makes journalists actors, not merely observers, and there is no escaping the responsibilities that accompany that role. British journalist (and later member of parliament) Martin Bell has argued that "in the news business it isn't involvement but indifference that makes for bad practice. Good journalism is the journalism of attachment. It is not only knowing, but also caring."[4]

In this context, one of journalism's most important roles is that of awakening the public's conscience. Journalists must decide when the alarm must be sounded and how best to do so.

Governments' Changing Outlook

News coverage generally reflects governments' views of foreign affairs. These are undergoing revision as Cold War principles recede into history. For the major democracies, particularly the United States, the task is twofold: to define what their world role should be, and to enlist domestic political support for that definition. At the heart of this matter, again especially for the United States, is deciding what to do with power.

During the Cold War, the answer was easy: stand firm and protect yourself and your allies against a formidable adversary. With that adversary gone, grand strategies change but the responsibilities of power remain.

Complicating matters is the issue of public resolve. A mix of idealism and fear provided a foundation of support for America's foreign policymakers when there was a superpower foe. That foundation wobbled sometimes, but it could usually be steadied through appeals to patriotism or reminders about nuclear menace.

Much danger remains, but it has assumed a different look: the threat of terrorism, or the disproportionate clout of a minor power (the "rogue state") with major weaponry. Responding to new threats is part of the business of being a modern world leader, but just possessing the ability to react falls far short of being a comprehensive foreign policy. For one thing, a country such as the United States presumably has room for some altruism in its dealings with the rest of the world. That can range from aiding a nation's economic growth to sending troops to help during a humanitarian emergency. This presumption about altruism depends on the existence of a willingness to act, which is a function of political leadership.

At the heart of this matter is the definition of "national interest." During the Cold War, that meant self-preservation and a vague notion of achieving and maintaining superiority in varied venues. With self-preservation no longer the same kind of pressing issue, and with "superiority" less relevant, a new philosophy needs to be articulated.

That need, however, may not be apparent to those politicians who prefer to manage crises on an ad hoc basis, and who like a policy-free flexibility that allows them to drift with the political winds. Perhaps they believe that such formlessness is wise until post–Cold War alignments become better defined, but meanwhile a leadership vacuum exists. The lack of a governing philosophy could be seen in the Bush administration's poorly thought-through response in 1992 to events in Somalia and President Bill Clinton's ambivalence about an American role in the Balkans, Rwanda, and elsewhere. If it were to rely on a strict definition of "national interest" grounded in security concerns, the United States would be able to remain distant from most of the conflicts boiling around the world. But no American administration is likely to adopt a doctrine of rigorous disengagement, if only for the loss of prestige that would accompany such a disavowal.

That still leaves the task of defining grounds for involvement. National interest is broadened by its incorporation of national values, and that can be the basis for stepping into a crisis. The form of participation can range from rhetoric to money to military force, any and all of which should be governed by a consistent philosophy.

Old-school pragmatists frown on what they consider to be the ill-considered moralistic interventionism of Madeleine Albright and others, and believe instead in the broad applicability of James Baker's observation about Yugoslavia as it was disintegrating: "We don't have a dog in that fight."[5] Along these lines, Henry Kissinger observed that "once the doctrine of universal intervention spreads and competing truths contest, we risk entering a world in which, in G. K. Chesterton's phrase, virtue runs amok."[6] Supporters of Albright's approach argue, however, that willingness to champion humanitarian causes is the mark of an enlightened foreign policy.

Neither side in this debate has the upper hand politically. American foreign policy remains strikingly inconsistent, and that infects the policies of America's allies. No one, friend or foe, seems to know if the United States might be willing to go beyond defending baseline security interests and move into protecting values, such as human rights. Even when a military course is selected, effectiveness is often limited by a refusal to endorse the fierceness and accept the casualties that are part of war. This has been referred to as a refusal to "cross the Mogadishu line," based on the post-Somalia Clinton administration doctrine that assigned highest priority to protecting American personnel.[7] As a result, writes Michael Ignatieff, the opponents of the Western democracies "reason that the West's commitment to human rights is canceled out by its unwillingness to take casualties, and its commitment to help the vulnerable is canceled out by its unwillingness to take and hold territory."[8]

Given that perceived lack of resolve, endorsement of humanitarian principles has limited impact. This pertains not just to the United

States, but also to NATO and to some extent to the United Nations. In addition to the unmatched sophistication of much of its weaponry, the U.S. military has unique intelligence-gathering and logistical capabilities (such as airlift capacity) that are crucial to any but the smallest and quickest military operations. So far, no American president has clearly stated the U.S. position on using these resources in humanitarian crises that arise from armed conflict. The United States, with NATO, responded to Serb aggression in Kosovo, but this was an ad hoc decision, not grounded in clearly defined policy and certainly not set forth as precedent for future actions.

This is not to say that there is no movement toward devising standards for humanitarian intervention. The United Nations Security Council resolution of April 24, 1992, cited "the magnitude of human suffering" in Somalia as a threat to peace and security. The previous standard for such an actionable threat had been a cross-border dispute between at least two sovereign states.[9] Journalist William Shawcross has written: "Increasingly among the rich West there is a belief that humanitarianism must now be part of national policymaking in a way which it has never been before. That conviction bestows a right to interference which cannot always be carried out, but sometimes should be. It is an ambitious doctrine, both morally and politically."[10]

Before an ambitious doctrine such as the one Shawcross cites is widely embraced, bureaucratic mindsets must change. Relief expert Andrew Natsios wrote that most U.S. policymakers "do not view humanitarian disaster assistance as a principal objective or undergirding principle of U.S. foreign policy. . . . Humanitarian interventionism does not have a large career constituency in the State or the Defense Department."[11]

The practical demands of humanitarian intervention are daunting. The pattern during the past decade has been to insert, at least initially, a small, lightly armed force. As a political gesture, this exudes nobility. As a way to halt human rights abuses, it borders on pointlessness. The monitors may end up watching terrible things happening while they lack the power to react. Those perpetrating the abuses are quick to see this, and they proceed as if the monitors were not even there. On some occasions, monitors are murdered (as in Rwanda) or taken hostage or ignored (as in Bosnia). Unwilling to risk being dragged into a conflict that will produce casualties among their personnel, the countries that have dispatched the monitors concern themselves mostly with crafting extraction plans so they can exit quickly if their representatives' safety is jeopardized.

At the very least, military personnel in such situations should be suitably armed and otherwise equipped so they can protect nonmilitary relief efforts designed to provide food, shelter, medical care, and clean water and sanitation to victims of war or other disasters.

Inadequately armed soldiers pose no threat and accomplish little. This is the kind of situation in which the news media might play a constructive role. By documenting what is going on and evaluating the impact of the monitors, journalists may influence public opinion, which in turn may get the attention of policymakers. If powerful countries insist on proceeding gingerly and resist taking on any significant policing duties, news coverage might provide a moral counterbalance to political inertia. Maybe the public will watch dispassionately as events unfold and be satisfied with limited intervention. On the other hand, maybe news coverage will stir the civic conscience, fueling outrage and generating pressure on policymakers.

News stories do not just appear and then evaporate; they can have effect, especially if they are done well. How much effect they have and what kind of results they produce will vary, but clearly the news media are not mere "observers" in the sense that they cannot influence the events they cover. The adage that the news media don't tell people what to think but what to *think about* is accurate. A corollary is that the effect of news coverage is not determinative in itself but is, along with other factors, influential.

Journalists' claims that they have no interest in outcomes are disingenuous. As a practical matter, objectivity is an illusion; choices about what to cover, as well as how to cover, are not made in a moral vacuum. Why bother doing journalism if there is no intent to provide the information that will affect how people think about things?

In domestic (mainly local) reporting, proponents of civic or public journalism have grappled with the balance between objectivity and involvement. Davis "Buzz" Merritt, who as editor of the *Wichita Eagle* was an early advocate of this approach to coverage, wrote, "If journalists are smart enough and professional enough to define some razor-thin line of objectivity and adhere to it, we are also smart enough and professional enough to define a slightly different line without tumbling all the way into the abyss of inappropriate involvement."[12] What is appropriate and what is inappropriate involvement remains open to debate, but civic journalism's commitment to fostering increased public participation in shaping policy need not be limited to domestic issues.

The extent of journalistic involvement is an old issue that takes on new significance in light of the changing political and military approaches to foreign crises. "Virtual war," for instance, has immense appeal to the political leaders of the countries capable of waging it. In brief, virtual war is combat that can be waged without incurring casualties while inflicting precisely targeted destruction on the enemy. The attacks on Serbia during the 1999 Kosovo war are an example of this. Using Cruise missiles and planes flying beyond the reach of Serb defenses, NATO (primarily the United States) was able to attack with impunity. The precision and effectiveness of this approach are debatable, but launching a virtual war clearly does not require the expenditure of political capital that traditional warfare demands.

When it was fought in 1991, the Persian Gulf War was called a modern war, with its high-tech weapons and live television coverage. But it really may have been a last gasp of the old-style warfare: amassing and sustaining a huge ground force to free an invaded country, with combat strategy that was expected to entail heavy casualties on both sides. In contrast, Kosovo was an air war, with the use of ground troops ruled out initially by NATO leaders who were uncertain of their constituents' support for the enterprise.

As appealing as this kind of combat may be to policymakers seeking public approval, it raises an important moral question that Michael Ignatieff asks in his book, *Virtual War*: "If military action is cost-free, what democratic restraints will remain on the resort to force?"[13] That is an issue for the news media as well as for governments because news coverage should dispel any sense of unreality that attaches to war and present the bloody truth that is the essence of even a virtual conflict. Martin Bell has written: "In our anxiety not to offend and upset people, we were not only sanitizing war but even *prettifying* it, as if it were an acceptable way of settling disputes, and its victims never bled to death but rather expired gracefully out of sight. How tactful of them, I thought. But war is real and war is terrible. War is a bad taste business."[14]

The press, then, has dual responsibilities: to call attention to situations in which governmental action—such as military intervention or non-military aid—may be appropriate, and to provide accurate descriptions of the results of policy, military or otherwise. This is not a redefinition of the news media's role. The task, as always in journalism, is to report the truth. That verges on the trite, but it is a more complex mandate than it might seem, especially given the political ambiguities and technological capabilities that affect policy today. Walter Lippmann wrote that "news and truth are not the same thing and must be clearly distinguished."[15] A country's leader may say, "Our borders have been violated." That statement is news, but is it true? Were the borders actually violated? The journalist's job is to report the news—in this case the statement—but also to report as much of the truth as can be discovered. The news by itself is not enough, and in some cases presenting "just the news" amounts to a dereliction of journalistic responsibility.

Taking Cues from Government

Just how much influence do the news media wield in the foreign policy-making process? In *Debating War and Peace*, Jonathan Mermin argued that media power may be overrated, and says that "the spectrum of debate in Washington . . . has determined the spectrum of debate in the news." He expands on this: "The reason the media have no independent impact on the foreign-policy debate is that journalists have ceded to *politicians* the power to set the spectrum of debate in the news. . . . The agenda-setting power journalists decline to exercise does not vanish into the air. Instead, it is passed on to politicians."[16]

Deferring to politicians may make sense because as a practical matter, these officials have real power, not the ethereal authority the news media might possess. Governments, not news organizations, can dispatch troops, provide economic assistance, and supply other aid. The press can prod, but government can act. When government is unresponsive or unimaginative, however, the news media should play a role in shaping the issues agenda. Post–Cold War threats such as nuclear proliferation, environmental deterioration, and the spread of infectious disease should be on that agenda. The news media can alert governments and the public to crises in the making or to an overlooked issue, and perhaps may spur a constructive response.

Finding evidence of war crimes is one such task. Speaking about this in May 2000, Secretary of State Madeleine Albright said that journalists "have an indispensable role to play in exposing atrocities and the criminal conduct that unleashes them." Journalists, she added, are "messengers of truth whose dispatches are our daily challenge."[17]

Governments are increasingly adroit in their dealings with news media messengers and the challenge they present. A lingering legacy of the Vietnam War, in terms of press-government relations, is that officials work especially hard to control news coverage during armed conflict. They bring considerable sophistication to the task. Overt censorship has been imposed occasionally, but usually the efforts at control are more subtle, although quite effective. Knowing, for instance, of CNN's and other networks' insatiable hunger for content, the Pentagon during the Gulf and Kosovo wars provided endless briefings and captivating video, all designed to deliver the "news" that the government thought appropriate.

Beyond trying to influence news content, some policymakers are sharply critical of how the news media approach foreign affairs. Henry Kissinger wrote that the "ubiquitous and clamorous media are transforming foreign policy into a subdivision of public entertainment. The intense competition for ratings produces an obsession with the crisis of the moment, generally presented as a morality play between good and evil [and] having a specific outcome, and rarely in terms of the long-range challenges of history. As soon as the flurry of excitement has subsided, the media move on to new sensations." When the journalists move on, said Kissinger, they often do so prematurely. The issues still merit news coverage, he said, because "the underlying trends continue, some of them becoming more unmanageable the longer they remain unresolved."[18]

At the heart of news organizations' efforts is the determination of what is "newsworthy." To a considerable degree, the public ascribes importance to items that are presented on the news media's menu. Readers, listeners, and viewers won't pick every one of these items, but they almost certainly will not ask for items *not* on the menu. If events in the Sudan are being covered by some major news organizations, at least some members of the audience will pay attention. But if those events do not receive mainstream coverage, they are unlikely even to intrude on the public's consciousness. Perhaps Web browsing will change this, as people go to new venues to find information. But at least for the foreseeable future, few people will do that.

Granted, if the U.S. government were to send troops to the Sudan, then of course coverage and public attention would increase. The real issue for journalists is what to do about those crises that their government decides—for whatever reason—are not worthy of substantive response. To what extent should that judgment affect news organizations' decisions about whether or how much to cover the situation?

There may be a tendency to think, "If the government doesn't believe that this is important, why should we?" This is a dangerous path to follow. Independent evaluations of newsworthiness are crucial to honest and effective journalism. Allowing news priorities to be dependent on policy priorities means surrendering intellectual autonomy. Taking cues from government policymakers is part of making everyday news judgments, but journalists should jealously protect their prerogative to move beyond reliance on such signals.

Another party to judging newsworthiness is the nongovernmental organization (NGO), such as a relief agency, which may play a quasi-governmental role during some crises. NGOs are particularly important when governments are slow to respond or choose not to provide assistance. They have their own strategies for dealing with the news media, because like governments they are intensely interested in public opinion. NGOs use media coverage to spur government action and stimulate the flow of money from private as well as government sources. This money helps those in need, and it sustains the agencies themselves.

The NGOs can be important in news gathering because relief agencies may have the best access to refugee camps and other crisis spots. When journalists arrive on the scene, they might find that an NGO has a monopoly on transportation, translators, safe water, and other necessities that make the agency seem irresistible as a de facto partner in shaping coverage.

Canadian media consultant Rick Grant, who has managed relief agencies' media relations, wrote that "there is a formal dance of intricate detail between UN officials, aid workers, reporters, and news managers." To supplement news from the field, wrote Grant, "information is being relayed to domestic media back home from head offices of the aid groups. News releases tailored for domestic interest flow on a daily basis, op-ed pieces are written, and interviews and news conferences are arranged for returning aid workers."[19] Any operation this sophisticated merits at least some wariness on the part of journalists who rely on it.

For reporters, dependence on an NGO carries with it the same risks as overreliance on government sources. The agency may be doing fine work, but it also may have its own agenda. Nobility of purpose does not rule out efforts to manipulate the media.

The Real-Time World

Live coverage enhances already powerful stories. The audience feels that it is present at the event, rather than merely hearing an after-the-fact report. The intense pressures of live reporting mean that journalists providing this kind of coverage may be particularly susceptible to becoming captive to the drama at hand. They may slip into emotive reporting. Worse, the lack of time for reflection and corroboration can produce errors of fact and emphasis.

Gripping live reports can be a great asset in holding an audience. The ripple effects, however, may prove unpredictable. The public's reaction to news may, to some degree, influence policymakers' response to that news. This is not a simple cause-and-effect formula; the issue is far more complex than that. Policy that is carefully considered and solidly built is resistant to the ebb and flow of emotions of the moment. But no impenetrable wall exists between news coverage and public policy.

Images of disaster have become common television fare, both sensitizing and desensitizing the audience, depending partly on how the stories are presented. A network anchor can exercise considerable power by carefully choosing words and tone of delivery, implicitly urging the audience to care and respond. Or the anchor can relegate the story to the ever-expanding daily news pile by treating the topic as trivial, referring to horror in an offhand way. Writing about the 1994 war in Rwanda, Philip Gourevitch observed: "The piled-up dead of political violence are a generic staple of our information diet these days, and according to the generic report all massacres are created equal: the dead are innocent, the killers monstrous, the surrounding politics insane or nonexistent. Except for the names and the landscape, it reads like the same story from anywhere in the world. . . . The stories flash up from the void and, just as abruptly, return there."[20]

Policymakers interested in their own political survival pay attention to the tone and substance of crisis coverage. If news is framed in a way that makes it unlikely to produce much public reaction, government officials may treat that coverage as just one of many sources of information, without much influence by itself. But if a story leads a network's newscast for several days or longer, with implicit or explicit emphasis on its importance, it is no longer merely information. It becomes a political force in itself and must be addressed accordingly. How much impact such a story has will vary, but it cannot be ignored.

Judgments about a story's newsworthiness are based on many factors, including news organizations' business criteria, which may have little in common with humanitarian concerns. Sending news crews to distant places can wreak havoc with a news division's budget. The return on such investment is generally expected to be minimal in terms of boosts in ratings or circulation. A cost-benefit analysis that relies wholly on economic criteria will probably produce negative results concerning foreign coverage. If the criteria used, however, are based on journalism's professional responsibilities, the results may be different. That dichotomy fuels much debate within the news business.

Despite budget constraints, television news organizations may find international stories attractive because of their visual appeal, horrific as it sometimes may be. Relief official Andrew Natsios observed that "the television medium is naturally drawn to events with a potential for striking photography, a characteristic of complex emergencies only in their later and more deadly stages. . . . By the time these scenes are sufficiently dramatic to attract attention, the time for intervention has usually passed."[21] Should this question of timeliness be a journalistic concern? A still-developing story may be difficult to tell, requiring much background information and speculation about what might happen next. But if one of journalism's roles is that of sentinel, news coverage should include early warnings about impending crises. Consistent news coverage will alert the public and policymakers about what may lie ahead, such as the famine that is likely to occur after several years of drought. Such timely journalism can prove invaluable to humanitarian efforts designed to alleviate suffering.

The television technology that fosters real-time coverage does little in itself to expand or enrich news content. The Internet, however, offers more than speed. Its virtually infinite capacity means that the traditional format-related limits on how much information can (or will) be presented—a particular problem in television journalism—are removed. Background, statistics, and historical context are among the elements of a story that now can regularly be provided, along with links that let news consumers get material directly from the same sources reporters use.

As for newspaper readers, Stephen Hess, in a study published in 1996, noted that "the newspaper industry almost requires us to move to certain large cities if we wish to be well informed about the state of the world."[22] This is no longer the case for many readers, thanks to the Internet. The world's best papers can now be read by anyone anywhere with time and inclination to browse the Web. Internet journalism is still in its early stages, but clearly it is expanding the information resources available to the public, policymakers, and news professionals. Daily news coverage of the Middle East, for instance, is supplemented on news organizations'

Web sites by a vast treasury of background material: maps, biographies, documents, opinion and analysis, and much more. Governments and interest groups also use the Web to promote their positions and make still more primary sources available.

The Internet alters the three-way dynamic among the news media, news consumers, and policymakers. Journalists can report more and the public can learn more. If, as Internet use grows, news organizations provide more information and the public takes advantage of this, governments may have to deal with political pressures that sometimes arise as by-products of expanded knowledge. In this context, as in others, information enhances democracy.

There is nothing new in the tension between those who report the news and those who govern, but the public's expanded ability to get information independently could profoundly change the relationship. People who dig for information on their own may be less accepting of what established news organizations and public officials offer, and may be more demanding about their government's performance.

In the world of unmediated media, the news consumer who wants to watch the world has plenty of online options:

- *Various news organizations.* The BBC, Reuters, China News Agency, Le Monde, and other news organizations from throughout the world, including small news agencies that can reach a greatly enlarged audience via the Internet (assuming that anyone finds them on the vast expanse of the Web).
- *Official sources.* Individual governments and organizations such as the United Nations, NATO, the CIA, and more. Nongovernmental organizations. Relief agencies, interest groups, and others.
- *Individuals.* Self-appointed spokespersons for causes and people caught up in events. During the 1999 war in Kosovo, Web sites and e-mail dispatches from all these categories were available, offering different perspectives on the fighting and the issues behind the conflict. The hardest thing about getting information from them was finding them on the Web, but some news organizations provided links to the more obscure sites. Verification of these electronic sources can be problematic. Are "witnesses" who claim they are providing firsthand accounts really who they say they are, or are they provocateurs and purveyors of disinformation?

Kosovo was the first Web war, a technological step forward comparable to Edward R. Murrow's radio broadcasts during the London blitz, television coverage from Vietnam, and live TV in the Persian Gulf War. A big difference between Kosovo and the rest was the amount of choice that members of the public had when deciding where to get the news. The limitations of the radio dial and television clicker are obsolete. Even the expanding spectrum of cable and satellite channels is no match for the Web.

What the public will do with all this newly available information is unknown. Given the technology at the disposal of the news media and the public, "I didn't know about that" will be a flimsy excuse when a crisis is brewing anywhere in the world. But availability of information is only part of the equation. The news consumer must choose to partake.

Using the Internet, if journalists go to the trouble spot of the moment, they can report immediately. Even if they cannot get there in person, they may be able to tap into local resources electronically. Without doubt, the news media can get lots of information. But they have to want to do so.

That has nothing to do with technology and everything to do with a sense of mission and the larger concept of professional responsibility. Professional responsibility should transcend the physical capabilities of the news business, but journalism has become increasingly entranced by its own gadgetry, whether it be a local television station's helicopter or a network's satellite access or a Web site that offers streaming video.

That said, the techniques of news gathering would benefit from some fine-tuning. Relief agency officials John Hammock and Joel Charny suggest that news organizations adopt a new approach for covering emergencies, taking steps such as these:

- Provide better training for journalists about the issues and cultures of countries they are sent to cover.
- Maintain greater independence from government agencies when determining the importance of international crises.
- Pay closer attention to semantics, using care when citing, for example, an "ethnic clash" led by "political leaders" in Europe while describing similar events in Africa as "tribal warfare" led by "warlords." The public takes cues from words; condescension or stereotyping–even if unintentional–can undermine the impact of a story.

- Report more about the ways people in the midst of a crisis are trying to help themselves. During an emergency, the victims are usually doing more than just awaiting rescue by outsiders. If their often heroic efforts were more widely recognized, relief assistance might become more likely. To keep the news audience's attention, it is useful to remember that people are interested in people. As a result, stories about people may be most effective in at least indirectly influencing policy.[23]

Undertaking such efforts as Hammock and Charny prescribe is not difficult. It does, however, require recognition that something more than parachute journalism—belated deployment of poorly prepared reporters—is required if the public is to gain more than a superficial understanding of the events being covered.

News and Money

Relatively few news executives appear willing to gamble that the American news audience might be interested in the rest of the world. They often adopt a lightweight approach to news that reduces many stories to soap opera. An "international story" is the Elian Gonzalez controversy, which was presented with heavy emphasis on drama and action, while neglecting larger policy matters. Even online news can be undermined by the "if it bleeds, it leads" mindset, which is frighteningly pervasive in many parts of the news business.

American news organizations have retreated from comprehensively covering the world beyond U.S. borders. In television, the big three broadcast networks—ABC, CBS, and NBC—have ceded overseas preeminence to CNN. As of late 1998, CNN had twenty-three foreign bureaus with corespondents, while ABC had five, CBS four, and NBC (with its sibling MSNBC) seven. Fox News Channel had five. The big three rely increasingly on partnerships with foreign networks, such as Japan's NHK and Germany's ZDF, plus international television news agencies such as Reuters Television and Associated Press Television News. In addition to maintaining its own bureaus, CNN has relationships with international partners, giving and receiving video.

The idea of international partnerships may sound good, but it has flaws. Reliance on others can limit the scope of independent editorial decision making. Former NBC executive Tom Wolzien said that sometimes when using overseas video services, "you start worrying about it. By the time the tape gets on the air, nobody has the foggiest idea who made it or whether the pictures were staged."[24] CBS correspondent Betsy Aaron told a Columbia University forum: "I don't believe that buying footage and looking at it second-hand is a substitute for going there yourself. I do know that when I look at the tape and I don't see what's beyond the tape, I am not seeing the story. I'm relying on someone else to gather that story for me. I have no idea what the person's agenda was—and there always is an agenda. And we're putting that on the air with the CBS label or the NBC label or the ABC label and we're doing it in cavalier fashion that we never would have done twenty years ago or ten years ago or even five years ago."[25]

Cutting corners eventually becomes visible. Studies conducted in the late 1990s found that American newspapers devoted 2 percent of their news space to foreign affairs stories, compared to slightly more than 10 percent in 1971. Of course, there must be some limits to what a news organization tries to cover. As *Washington Post* ombudsman E. R. Shipp noted about her newspaper, even with 25 foreign correspondents selectivity is necessary. "The emphasis," she wrote, "is on news that can be anticipated, including elections, international conferences, and papal or presidential visits; locales that correspondents can get to in a timely fashion; and events or trends with major implications for life in these United States."[26]

Television newscasts devoted half as much time to international events in 1999 as they did in 1989. As for weekly newsmagazines, international news constituted 13 percent of content in 1995, compared to 22 percent in 1985.[27] *Newsweek* editor Maynard Parker reported that putting a foreign subject on the cover meant a 25 percent drop in newsstand sales.[28] In 1997, *Time* had one foreign news cover, besides the two in a row it ran after the death of Princess Diana, compared to the eleven it had run in 1987.[29]

This shrinkage happened gradually; stories became shorter and more newsworthy events went uncovered. Few news consumers seemed to notice and even fewer complained. Lack of "audience demand" is a useful rationale when undercutting the intellectual content of news. That such an excuse is patronizing rarely deters news organizations from using it. Television news practices have had a particularly pernicious effect. In his study of international news coverage (using data from 1992 and earlier), Stephen Hess found that newspapers were reporting from roughly twice the number of countries that TV reported from. Hess said, "Television news creates a much simpler map of the world than its newspaper counterparts."[30] With much of the mass audience relying primarily on television, that simpler map is still the one most frequently consulted.

CNN is an exception, largely because of its international audience. Before the 1991 Gulf War, CNN (as CNNI–CNN International) reached about 10 million households outside the United States. By the time of the Kosovo War in 1999, that number had risen to 150 million.[31] Many of these viewers are very interested in news from throughout the world, so the network provides it.

Comprehensive foreign news coverage requires a substantial commitment of personnel and equipment, and extravagant costs are often incurred when covering events in distant locales. When the press corps descends on a place such as Albania, as happened during the war in neighboring Kosovo, prices for hotel rooms, rental cars, and food will skyrocket. For a big story, news organizations will find the money. But having a permanent bureau in a city such as Paris will cost a lot and produce relatively few stories for an audience that supposedly prefers "news you can use."

A growing number of news organizations have been swallowed in mergers and other acquisitions, often ending up with a new parent company that has little interest in news except as a moneymaker. Commitment to journalistic standards sometimes is compromised when news organizations become parts of vast non-news conglomerates. The "big three" American networks are among the examples of this: ABC is owned by Disney, CBS by Viacom, and NBC by General Electric. These might be fine companies, but they are not grounded in the traditions of public service that should be an integral part of journalism. That is one reason that corporate number crunchers may be quick to target spending on international coverage.

Despite the allure of cutting expenses, the reasoning behind limiting the scope and substance of international coverage is fundamentally flawed. Survey research has determined that many news consumers are interested in what is going on overseas. Pew Center polls have found international news ranking ahead of sports and national politics. A readership survey for *USA Today* discovered that international coverage is a key factor in shaping reader loyalty. Knight Ridder research found that readers think newspapers have gone overboard on local news and cite lack of international news as a major reason for being dissatisfied with their papers.[32]

Although the amount of coverage is not in itself the determinative measure of solid journalism, it is a starting point when evaluating news organizations' performance. If coverage is skimpy, then qualitative judgments are pointless. So, "good foreign coverage" must begin with a willingness to devote a reasonable percentage of the news product to global news. Defining "reasonable" is the next task.

This commitment need not be onerous. Even the laments about costs do not ring true, particularly for newspapers. They can easily find basic international news if they want it. Most of them already pay for it as part of the Associated Press service that virtually every American paper of any size subscribes to. That, said veteran foreign correspondent Peter Arnett, "is the discouraging reality the AP must face. It puts out a superb international news report . . . that's hardly being touched." Arnett also argued that "building in one additional page a day to beef up a paper's existing international coverage would cost a fraction of one percent of its operating expenses, yet would do much to ensure a foreign report that at least touches all the bases."[33]

If audience interest and cost are not blocking coverage of the world, what is? One factor is collective inertia within the news business. Faced with a dramatically different world since the end of the Cold War, many news organizations have not made the effort needed to understand a system of politics that is more shaded with nuance than was the stark face-off between superpowers. When the possibility of nuclear cataclysm was the reliably frightening backdrop for much international news, the drama on which the news media thrive was always present, as was a formulaic good-guys-versus-bad-guys approach to stories. Of course, this was absurdly simplistic, but it could be understood by journalists and their audiences alike.

Whether the story was about Latin America, Africa, Southeast Asia, or almost anywhere else, relevance could always be presumed, even if grounded in shaky assumptions about "client states" acting as the superpowers' proxies. The public understood, at least in a superficial way, the stakes of the Cold War. Journalism likes a stark contrast between good and evil, even if that delineation is more a matter of perception than reality. Shorthand references, such as "Soviet-inspired" or "pro-American," make storytelling easy, although the stories may be misleadingly one-dimensional.

The geopolitical alignments of the early twenty-first century lend themselves even less to precise line-drawing. Some long-term enmities are clearly defined, such as that between India and Pakistan or Israel and Syria, as are some friendships, such as that between the United States and Great Britain. But as increased autonomy replaces traditional unions and alliances, and as the sanctity of physical borders is challenged, identities become blurred, at least to the eyes of casual observers. In the Balkans, are the Kosovars part of greater Serbia or greater Albania? In Sierra Leone, what is the distinction between a "freedom fighter" and a rapacious thug? Might NATO undertake military operations without authorization from the United Nations, and if so, how far beyond its member countries' borders might it venture? Even more parochial matters, such as the definition of "American interests," are fluid in the absence of the Cold War's frame of reference.

Such issues challenge policymakers, academic experts, and the news media, especially journalists whose penchant for terseness does not mesh well with complex politics. This is particularly the case with television news. An American air assault on Baghdad or Belgrade is perfect; it is presented as a graphic depiction of good guys versus bad guys. Why those assaults are taking place and what their effects might be are very different matters, and a simple explanation can quickly slip into being an inaccurate one.

On a cautiously optimistic note, news media convergence may bring additional substance to coverage. Television news organizations, for instance, will offer online supplements to their traditionally brief, video-oriented presentations. Print media will add video and audio—real-time when the occasion demands—to their online reports and analyses. With the Web's vast capacity, much more information will be available to journalists as well as to news consumers. Reporters can gather material from the Web sites of governments, organizations, and individuals. Research can be conducted more thoroughly as well as more quickly. Journalists' task will be to sort through the huge amount of information that is accessible online and give the public some guidance about relative importance. Cataloguing what is available and packaging the news in non-linear ways, with links to primary sources and background details, are evolving crafts that will redefine the news product.[34]

For their part, news consumers must decide how much "news" they really want. Many people have neither the time nor the desire to digest encyclopedic journalism on a daily basis. They have become accustomed to skimming headlines and glancing at video. To get them to plunge into deeper waters, news organizations must make their product interesting. Aside from the obvious issues related to ratings and circulation, if the news product fails to attract an audience, what is the point of presenting it? Merely gathering information and making it available is not journalism. Storytelling is an important ingredient. The best reporters and editors know that they must make the news both understandable and memorable.

The last decade of the twentieth century offered striking examples of how the presence and absence of news coverage may affect millions of lives. Journalism does matter. Now, as foreign policy evolves apace with the world's changing political realities, journalism must likewise continue to transform itself. The diverse issues raised in this chapter suggest how demanding this transformation will be. Later chapters will examine these matters in more detail.

The evolution of journalism is not a matter of communications theory or academic definitions of "gatekeeping." It transcends ratings and circulation competition. Because of the news media's effects—even if limited—on public opinion and public policy, deciding what stories to cover and how to cover them is a fundamental ethical issue.

CHAPTER TWO

✣

Tearing down Walls:
History Begins Anew

The post–Cold War era began with a splendid media event. On November 9, 1989, the East German government announced that its citizens no longer needed permission to leave the country. The Berlin Wall suddenly ceased to be a barrier to freedom, and tens of thousands of Germans surged back and forth between both sides of the divided city. Historians Michael Beschloss and Strobe Talbott described the grand celebration: "Jazz bands played under searchlights originally installed to help catch fugitives. East and West Berliners leapt atop the ugly twenty-eight-year-old partition, raising glasses of champagne and beer, they sang, danced, hacked off pieces of the wall and wept with joy."[1]

Television covered the festivities live, with the big three American networks dispatching their anchormen to report from the scene. Cameras also were taken into the Oval Office, where President George Bush appeared reluctant to join the celebration. That earned him criticism from some journalists and politicians as being unappreciative of the magnitude of what was happening. On several occasions, he said, "I'm not going to dance on the wall."[2] Bush had decided that as important as the events in Germany were, gloating about them would be taking a cheap shot at the precariously situated Mikhail Gorbachev and could damage U.S.–Soviet relations. Bush put policy ahead of performance, an uncommon practice among politicians in the television age.

Even without the president's participation, the show continued. This was politics as festival, and the news media reveled in it.

The crumbling of the Berlin Wall and other changes accompanying the end of the Cold War meant that the news media, like other institutions, had to redefine basic practices and adjust priorities. News executives had viewed the geopolitical situation in much the same way that policymakers had: a bipolar planet divided into "the free world" and "the communist world." Although simplistic, those labels influenced a half-century of news coverage.

Policymakers, the news media, and the public were presented with the opportunity to redefine, or at least reiterate, the political and ethical standards that govern international relations. The various players in the foreign policy process could establish new priorities: what interests and values were to be most important. These are matters that concern the news media as well as policymakers. Those who cover the news, like those who govern, must allocate finite resources and possess a sense of mission.

The public's opinion about the world also was changing, as old hopes and fears gave way to new ones. How the public viewed the world would, as always, affect how foreign affairs officials and global journalists would do their jobs.

During the Cold War, the newsworthiness of individual countries and their leaders was largely determined by their relationship to the United States and the Soviet Union. Reporting reinforced the conventional wisdom of the moment concerning the players in the superpower-dominated great game. This was usually very orderly. Occasionally a Tito or a Nehru would puzzle journalists as well as policymakers, but most nations and their leaders could be neatly categorized, making life easy for journalists and their audience.

By the early 1990s, even the staunchest proponents of this convenient formula had to admit that it was obsolete. Leading news organizations began to reshape their foreign reporting. At the *New York Times* in 1992, foreign editor Bernard Gwertzman, in a memo to his staff, wrote: "In the old days, when certain countries were pawns in the Cold War, their political orientation alone was reason enough for covering them. Now with their political orientation not quite as important, we don't want to forget them, but we have an opportunity to examine the different aspects of a society more fully."[3]

In addition to changes in reporting about individual countries, the general topics of coverage expanded. Security issues became less important as the threat of nuclear war diminished. In the late 1990s, globalization was getting more attention, even though many people were uncertain exactly what it meant. New technologies fostered economic growth that brought even greater wealth to the United States and other developed nations. This expansion of wealth seemed capable of reaching places that had never known prosperity. The Internet and genome research were among the revolutionary manifestations of progress that were reshaping the world and providing new material for the news media.

When the focus of news coverage shifts from destroying life to enhancing and understanding life—going from missiles to modems, from Dr. Strangelove to Dr. Crick—the job of the journalist changes enormously. Much new information must be mastered, which involves learning the substance of new issues and acquiring new sources. Defining relative newsworthiness is another challenge—deciding what goes on page one, leads a newscast, or tops a Web page. The overall tone of the news may also evolve, reflecting promise rather than dread.

This is not to say that all the news is rosy. Low-level proliferation of atomic weaponry continues. Some American politicians remain fixated on the notion of a "rogue state" attack on the United States, either through conventional means such as a missile or—more likely—with the weapon delivered in a terrorist's suitcase. Another possibility is a nuclear conflict that does not directly involve the United States, such as a war between India and Pakistan. There is also much non-nuclear carnage around the world, such as genocide in Africa and barbarism in the Balkans. War correspondents can always find work.

Defining the News

Reshaping coverage requires systemic change in the news business, beginning with a redeployment of resources. Today "the news" is much more scattered, with important stories on any given day emerging not from Washington or Moscow, but from Pyongyang, Lima, and Freetown. American audiences, according to those who run the news business, are little interested in the goings-on in such locales unless they can be shown that events there have a direct, substantive impact on their own lives.

This presumed lack of interest is a convenient disincentive to restructuring international news gathering in ways that would foster the comprehensive, interesting coverage needed if people are to make sense of the ways the world is changing. David Halberstam wrote about this: "When the Berlin Wall came down, the one thing I never thought of was the effect it would have on journalism, television journalism in particular, releasing those who ran the network news shows from their obligations to cover the world, and allowing them instead to hold a mirror up to an increasingly self-obsessed society."[4]

With the growth of online news, debate about what the news audience wants has intensified. News organizations can precisely measure audience members' interest: which Web pages they read and how long they spend doing so. Internet users can even design custom news services to deliver information about the topics that most interest them. This process also can be easily monitored by news organizations. If news executives determine that news consumers' Web habits indicate that Americans care little about international news, that can then be used to justify limiting overseas coverage.

This muddled approach to international news is especially unfortunate because it ignores the news media's responsibility to provide the public with important information. If the public appears uninterested in foreign news, that should be seen by journalists as a challenge to make coverage more relevant and interesting. As journalists redraw their maps of the world, they should do so with ambitious precision and breadth, bringing into the scope of coverage those nations and peoples who for too long have remained beyond the purview of the news.

Technology and Coverage

George Washington University Professor Steven Livingston has suggested that "in a fashion suggestive of the way the printing press 500 years ago undermined the position of the Catholic Church as a mediating institution between heaven and Earth, the creation of global, real-time television has undermined the diplomat's ability to mediate between distant events and the public."[5] Much diplomacy is now visible not just to an inner circle of policymakers, but also to the attentive news consumer. Diplomats who believe that their work is due a certain reverence are likely to view journalists as heathens who trample on the niceties of the diplomatic arts. Journalists might consider that a compliment.

Policymakers who cherish orderliness may see much news coverage, especially real-time reporting, as little more than mischief-making.

The argument can be made that in the rush to get the story first, important facts are not corroborated or explained, leaving many stories deeply flawed. Even if the basics are right, the complexities and nuances so important in international affairs are likely to be glossed over or ignored altogether.

Those criticisms may have merit, but the case can also be made that the policy process is inherently lethargic and is so constrained by bureaucratic politics that it is insensitive to real human issues. The news media, therefore, play an invaluable role by bringing a sense of urgency to that process.

The much ballyhooed "CNN effect" is presumed to illustrate the dynamic tension that exists between real-time television news and policy-making, with the news having the upper hand in terms of influence. In a nutshell, the CNN effect can be defined this way: televised images, especially heart-wrenching pictures of suffering civilians, will so stir public opinion that government officials will be forced to adjust policy to conform to that opinion. There is a certain logic to the theory, and it cheers journalists who like to think they are powerful, but there is a fundamental problem: It just ain't so, at least not as a straightforward cause-and-effect process.

News coverage, real-time and otherwise, may have high emotional content (this is especially true of television news) that can capture the attention of the public, which may put pressure on policymakers. That pressure usually has to do with the most visible events of the moment—as presented by the news media—rather than the more complex and, in the long run, more significant issues. When such news stories appear, governments try to insulate their policy processes from the pressures the coverage can generate. They usually succeed at this. British journalist Nik Gowing, who studies the effects of real-time news on foreign policy, has observed that such coverage may affect the personal emotions of policymakers but not policy itself, except in instances of "policy panic"—the rare occasions on which policymakers allow the news to become determinative rather than merely influential.[6]

British scholar Stephen Badsey got it right when he wrote that "although the CNN effect may happen, it is unusual, unpredictable, and part of a complex relationship of factors."[7] The news *does* affect people, and sometimes they do respond. Coverage of the 1984 Ethiopian famine spurred an outpouring of aid from the public and then from governments. Reports about the plight of Iraqi Kurds at the end of the Gulf War pushed the United States and its allies toward establishing a safe haven to protect the Kurds from Saddam Hussein. Television pictures of refugees pouring from Kosovo into Albania helped win public support in the United States for the bombing of Serbia. There are further instances such as these, but individually or collectively they do not constitute definitive evidence of a consistent causal relationship between news coverage and policymaking.

The coverage may strengthen or weaken the public's backing for a given policy, but that is just one of many political factors that government officials contend with. Michael Ignatieff wrote that "war does not become illegitimate simply because citizens see carnage on their screens. It becomes illegitimate when the political reasons for it no longer convince."[8] This echoes one of the wiser observations about the Vietnam War. Clark Clifford, secretary of defense during the latter part of Lyndon Johnson's presidency, said that the potency of news coverage was overrated in terms of its effects on public opinion. "Reporters and the antiwar movement," he wrote, "did not defeat America in Vietnam. Our policy failed because it was based on false premises and false promises. Had the results in Vietnam approached, even remotely, what Washington and Saigon had publicly predicted for many years, the American people would have continued to support their government."[9]

In policymaking, politics is more important than news stories. Writing about the deaths of 150,000 people during warfare in Burundi in the mid-1990s, Nik Gowing noted that the television coverage (which was not extensive) "did not overcome the new international instinct of caution that is driven by negligible political will and national interest."[10]

Perhaps both the level of slaughter and the amount of coverage must reach a hard-to-define critical mass before the public and policymakers take note. And even then, politics will usually prevail. If a nation's foreign policy is well defined and well defended by the officials responsible for it, it is unlikely to be blown hither and yon by the winds of news coverage. As ABC anchorman Peter Jennings has noted, "political leadership trumps good television every time. As influential as television can be, it is most influential in the absence of decisive political leadership."[11]

This is a crucial point. In most instances, the "CNN effect" will take hold only if a policy vacuum exists. In such cases, the impact of news coverage is magnified, and therefore so is journalistic responsibility. CNN correspondent Christiane Amanpour wrote that during these situations there is an increased burden on journalists in the field "to act responsibly, to weigh what we do or say, to understand that in these dangerous situations words we utter matter and can have consequences."[12]

The question of media impact has become more complicated with the increasing use of the Internet as information disseminator. If it reaches a large enough audience, material presented on Web sites of relief agencies and other private organizations involved in foreign affairs can affect public opinion and policy. The site of the International Rescue Committee in 2001, for example, had Web pages filled mostly with text and some photographs. As Web offerings become more sophisticated, groups such as the IRC could easily add audio and video material from their project sites. This content will reach the public directly and also will be picked up by news organizations for use in their own reports. Such information will prod news organizations and perhaps governments to pay attention to situations that otherwise may have been neglected.

Defining a Mission

Regardless of the effect news might have on policy, the journalist's job remains that of finding the truth and telling it. The mere existence of the journalistic voice is important. Rony Brauman, former head of Médecins sans Frontières, wrote that "silence always feeds oppression. Although knowing about a crisis does not solve it, the knowledge does at least pave the way for the most basic act of justice. If the guilty cannot be punished, then at least the victims can be recognized."[13]

The journalistic voice must be persistent. News organizations may be tempted to turn away from a story once its most sensational aspects have been reported. After the blood has been mopped up, what more is there? The rest of the story should be told. There *are* successes in international affairs: policies sometimes work; wrongs sometimes get righted. Nic Gowing wrote, "As the sharp drop in media coverage of IFOR's military success in Bosnia illustrated during 1996, coverage of 'unsexy' nation building and development projects, or the kind of economic regeneration efforts required to avoid conflict, is likely to be negligible at best."[14]

Against a backdrop of political and social change as the post–Cold War world sorts itself out, the news business finds itself in a continuing struggle to define its own role. Indications of "progress" around the world conflict with evidence of retrograde behavior, particularly in human rights matters. A journalist can make a good case that basic decency requires aggressive advocacy on behalf of those who cannot speak for themselves. If that premise is accepted, the next task is to reconcile that moral judgment with the standards of fairness and objectivity that are the heart of journalistic process.

Political Morality and the New World Order

Journalists benefit from studying the history and process of foreign policymaking. Unless news coverage is grounded in sophisticated appreciation of how a nation shapes its international priorities, that coverage is likely to be simplistic.

As it sets its priorities, the United States has tried to specify where it does *not* want to be involved. Warren Christopher, speaking about Bosnia, called the fighting there "a problem from hell" and said it "does not affect our vital national interests except as we're concerned about humanitarian matters and except as we're trying to contain it."[15] Christopher also said of Bosnia that "at heart, this is a European problem." Such efforts to distance the United States from overseas crises recall the observation of British diplomat Harold Nicolson, who, writing about the end of World War I, said that "America, eternally protected by the Atlantic, desired to satisfy her self-righteousness while disengaging her responsibility."[16]

Today, American ambivalence remains, giving way occasionally to spurts of activism. Henry Kissinger wrote, "In launching itself for the third time in this century on creating a new world order, America's dominant task is to strike a balance between the twin temptations inherent in its exceptionalism: the notion that America must remedy every wrong and stabilize every dislocation, and the latent instinct to withdraw into itself."[17]

Uncertainty about the extent of any unilateral U.S. commitment to other parts of the world has left the United Nations and NATO, and prospectively the European Union, as would-be police officers. If the United States chooses not to participate, military efforts will often reach only a level of marginal competence. With much uncertainty existing about American intentions, the "new world order"—which never has been coherently defined—is not very orderly. Even when the United States does engage, such as leading NATO in the fighting over Kosovo, U.S. political resolve may diminish quickly, leaving others to tidy up after the fighting stops or at least slows. One United Nations official remarked about Kosovo, "It was a NATO war; it will be a U.N. peace."[18]

But the United Nations' military prowess is questionable. General Francis Briquemont, who commanded UN forces in Bosnia in 1993, complained about the "fantastic gap between the resolutions of the Security Council, the will to execute these resolutions, and the means available to commanders in the field."[19]

Even within the United Nations, priorities are often unclear. Boutros Boutros-Ghali challenged the Eurocentric priorities of the Security Council, pointing out the willingness to fight what he called "a rich man's war" in the Balkans while letting much larger wars go unchecked in Africa.

NATO, although possessing considerable (mostly American) punch, also has its critics. With its narrowly defined mission—the defense of Western Europe—NATO has been labeled "the rich world's private army." How far NATO's mission really extends is open to debate. Protecting Persian Gulf oil seemed important enough to secure NATO members' individual participation in the American-led Gulf War coalition. Closer to home, the cycle of viciousness in the Balkans is a more direct challenge to NATO's resolve. Exasperation with American vacillation, coupled with recognition of U.S. dominance within NATO, has led Tony Blair and others to nibble at the issue of a European-only military capability. So far, the most enthusiastic supporters of this idea have been weapons manufacturers (many of them American) who believe that the more armies the better. Lacking adequate funds and leadership, proponents of a post-NATO force may have to wait until the United States demonstrates even greater aversion to European duties before making real progress toward their goal.

The enigmatic performance of the United States has drawn sharp criticism. *Foreign Affairs* managing editor Fareed Zakaria wrote: "Today it is not the world that has given up on America but America that has given up on the world. Historians will surely look back on this decade and be struck that at America's moment of greatest global triumph—when all the world looked to Washington for leadership—and in the midst of an almost-unprecedented economic boom, Americans became uncharacteristically small-minded in their ambitions."[20]

Predicting the inclinations of the United States becomes more difficult as U.S. military technology races farther ahead of that of the rest of the world. American weaponry has reached the point that the United States can inflict massive damage on most adversaries with little fear of incurring substantial—or perhaps even any—casualties. The Gulf War showed off American superiority in fighting what was primarily a conventional war, but that performance now can be viewed as an anachronism. The air war unleashed during the 1999 Kosovo war better illustrates American dominance. American aircraft (with help from NATO allies) inflicted substantial, if not decisive, damage on the Serbs with no U.S./NATO personnel lost.

The significance of such military accomplishments in this kind of war is debatable. Using high-tech weapons to destroy antiquated trucks makes little sense. Ground forces (and lower-flying aircraft) would have been more effective in wrecking the Serb military, but that would have involved U.S./NATO casualties.

The mode of war affects overall strategy. In future cases, the ability to wage war with relative impunity might provide incentive to intervene. Even a cautious American president may find this to be the best of all worlds: the ability to act forcefully with little political risk.

The moral issues of this kind of combat are more complex than the political ones. Commenting on "virtual war," Michael Ignatieff wrote: "Technological mastery removed death from our experience of war. But war without death—to our side—is war that ceases to be fully real to us."[21] For those on the receiving end, however, there is nothing unreal about war, virtual or otherwise. One-sidedness in combat efficiency changes the political, not the moral, elements of war. That is an issue that the news media should bring to the public's attention.

As international political standards evolve, two focal points are the United Nations and the United States. Kofi Annan has offered a credo that may be useful to both: "Impartiality does not and must not mean neutrality in the face of evil."[22] The words are noble, but resolve to back them up has been inconsistent. Particularly from the U.S. standpoint, the absence today of threats to "the national interest"—which could be detected whenever convenient during the Cold War—has made de facto neutrality appealing, no matter what evil might be present. Inaction usually carries no political penalty. The exception, according to Michael Ignatieff, occurs when shame is articulated "by a vocal minority of influential activists—with access to the media."[23]

This brings the debate about involvement versus disengagement back to the role of the news media. If public passion is to be roused, the news media will provide the stimulus, acting on their own initiative or giving voice to others. Policymakers may resist this stimulus, but they dare not ignore it.

Public Opinion

In the United States, public opinion about America's role in the world has long been the topic of debate. Some data are offered as proof that Americans are basically isolationist, and other evidence is cited as proof that Americans are fundamentally internationalist. Sometimes different interpretations of the same numbers are cited by partisans on opposite sides of the argument.

Policymakers tend to assume that the public is uninterested or negatively disposed toward overseas activism by the United States. But in their 1999 book *Misreading the Public: The Myth of a New Isolationism*, University of Maryland scholars Steven Kull and I. M. Destler wrote: "The key finding of this study is that this perception of the public as wanting the United States to disengage from the world is indeed widespread in the policy community, but that it is not sustained by empirical research. . . . In short, there is a significant gap between the dominant perceptions of public attitudes held by the policy community and the attitudes held by the majority of the American public."[24]

Another study, this one conducted in 1995 by Andrew Kohut and Robert C. Toth, also found that "Americans remain internationalist rather than isolationist," and reported that 60 percent of its poll respondents disagreed with the proposition that the United States "should go its own way in international matters." But Kohut and Toth noted that "this was the lowest level of disagreement in thirty years."[25]

Back to Kull and Destler: "Trend line polls show no decline in support for international engagement. At the same time, a majority also rejects the dominant world leader role for the United States that many policy practitioners thought the public endorsed. Rather, the public supports much greater emphasis on cooperative and multilateral forms of international involvement in which the United States contributes its 'fair share' along with other countries."[26]

Bounce back and forth among studies such as these and some consistent points become apparent. The public is *not* isolationist but nevertheless is very cautious about committing resources (and, in military matters, lives), especially on a unilateral basis. The Kohut and Toth study found that "the public wants U.S. foreign policy to serve its domestic agenda," including matters such as protecting U.S. jobs and strengthening the American economy.[27] That attitude seems to have found ready acceptance by elected officials, who are adept at praising generosity and parochialism in the same speech.

Other studies also reflect the public's cautious approach to internationalism. The Pew Research Center's 1997 report, "America's Place in the World II," found that since the mid-1970s a majority of Americans had disagreed with the idea that "the United States should mind its own business internationally." In September 1997, the margin was 54 percent to 39 percent in opposition to that premise.[28] A survey conducted by the Gallup Organization in late 1998 for the Chicago Council on Foreign Relations found that 61 percent of the public supported an active U.S. role in the world, and that 50 percent of the public believed that America was playing a more important and powerful role as a world leader than it had ten years before.[29] The Pew Center survey, however, found that just 35 percent of the public agreed that the U.S. role had expanded.[30]

The Chicago Council's survey also found the public to be decidedly in favor of multilateralism. By a margin of 72 percent to 21 percent, respondents said that the United States should not take action alone when responding to an international crisis. When asked if the United States should participate in UN peacekeeping missions, 57 percent agreed, up from 51 percent in 1994.[31] This survey asked respondents about the use of U.S. troops, even in a multilateral force, in a number of hypothetical situations, such as Iraq invading Saudi Arabia and Russia invading Poland. In none of the cases did a majority of respondents support U.S. military intervention.[32] The Pew Center poll asked similar questions and received generally similar answers. If South Korea were invaded, 58 percent favored intervention, 54 percent favored helping an invaded Saudi Arabia, and narrow pluralities opposed the use of U.S. forces in other scenarios.[33] The Kohut-Toth analysis found mixed feelings about American participation in UN military operations:

- 63 percent of respondents approved of sending U.S. troops as part of a UN force to assist in famine relief in Africa or Asia.
- 52 percent favored such a force being deployed "to prevent slaughters" in regional conflicts.
- 47 percent approved and 46 percent disapproved of sending a UN/U.S. force to Africa or Asia "to restore law and order."
- 46 percent approved and 47 percent disapproved of using such a force "to keep the peace when two sides in a conflict have called a truce."[34]

Participation in a UN force is one thing, but sustaining casualties is something very different, at least according to the conventional wisdom accepted by many policymakers. But Duke University professors Peter D. Feaver and Christopher Gelpi looked at survey data from 1998 and concluded that the polling results "suggest that a majority of the American people will accept combat deaths—so long as the mission has the potential to be successful. The public can distinguish between suffering defeat and suffering casualties."[35]

News coverage is also thought to affect public support when American troops are incurring casualties. But that assumption also may be too simplistic. The Kohut-Toth study found that "American casualties do have a profound impact on public support when the public feels the United States has little national interest at stake in the mission. But there is no evidence for deciding at what level the televised images of American casualties become intolerable if the public has concluded that U.S. national interests or some other larger reason justified the intervention."

The public generally rallies behind a presidential decision to use force, and that attitude "is reinforced by the extraordinary amounts of news coverage given to American forces committed to a foreign mission."[36] Particularly in the early stages of intervention, much of the coverage is resolutely boosterish. This is especially true of coverage by local news organizations, which thrive on human interest stories about "our" troops and which are provided ample assistance from the Pentagon, sometimes including free trips to the crisis scene.

The role of the news media in shaping opinions about foreign policy has also received attention from researchers. The Chicago Council's 1998 survey asked about interest in news coverage and found that only 29 percent of respondents were interested in news about other countries, while 45 percent were interested in U.S. relations with other countries. These were the lowest figures in almost twenty years.[37] Lack of interest and lack of knowledge also were found in the Kohut and Toth study, which cited surveys in the United States, Germany, and Japan and reported that "the task of winning support for international policies—indeed, for even articulating them coherently to the skeptical public—is more difficult in the United States than in the other nations surveyed because Americans know less about the world (and perhaps even less about the world than their parents did)."[38]

Along these lines, Richard Clark and Kenneth Dautrich, of the University of Connecticut's Center for Survey Research, found that "the public is neither isolationist nor internationalist. Rather, public opinion tends to be soft and amorphous, ready and willing to be shaped by both events and leadership. . . . The public holds deep convictions in certain domestic policy areas. . . . Matters of foreign policy, on the other hand, generally seem remote and public attention is episodic at best, uninformed at worst. Consequently, public opinion in the area of foreign policy tends to be shaped by external forces; the public looks to political elites and the media for leadership on foreign policy issues."[39]

The portrait emerging from these and similar surveys is that of a cautious and not particularly well-informed American public that values American prestige but is wary about the costs entailed when America asserts its power. This attitude is too soft to be called isolationism but is firm enough to force policymakers to present a solid case for military deployment or other overseas commitments. Intervention, especially on a unilateral basis, is hard to sell.

For journalists, the research findings underscore the importance of news coverage. The news must be presented in a way that will attract and hold the attention of an audience that has limited interest in reports about the rest of the world. When it is successful in doing that, the coverage may well affect public opinion about the events and issues being covered. News organizations should take this task seriously.

How Public Opinion Is Influenced

When the public is deciding about the political and moral aspects of a foreign policy issue, particularly during a crisis, the leadership exercised by the president and the tone and substance of congressional debate are crucial. When a president clearly and convincingly makes the case for action and when congressional leaders transcend partisanship, the public is likely to be supportive. How long that support lasts depends largely on how long effective political leadership continues.

The most significant influence of news coverage on public opinion at such times is grounded in how it reflects these matters–how the president and Congress are portrayed and how their actions relate to coverage from overseas of the crisis itself. George Bush learned in 1991 about the peril of dissonance between presidential behavior and news coverage of a humanitarian emergency. Relaxing after the end of the Gulf War, Bush was shown on television at a Florida golf course refusing to answer questions about Saddam Hussein's attacks on Kurdish refugees. The same newscasts presented video of the refugees trying to survive in the frigid mountains between Iraq and Turkey. The contrasting images contributed to a shift in public opinion in favor of helping the Kurds, which was promptly followed by a shift in U.S. policy.[40] The news media (especially television) are adept at personalizing a story–defining issues with human faces, not abstractions. People are interested in people, so when the news audience sees a tormented refugee or a wounded child, foreign policy becomes not "mere politics," but a matter of human interest.

Policymakers pay attention not only to hard news reports but also to editorials, columns, and other commentary. Jack Matlock, who served as American ambassador to the Soviet Union during the Reagan administration, wrote that "what the press commentary tells you is not so much what the decision should be, but how much trouble you may have with the American public and with Congress over an issue. It's not that you read editorials to make policy, but the editorials are data in understanding your own public and, of course, in understanding how the media will present these issues."[41]

In the relationship between government and news media, part of the task for journalists is to resist inertia and search for the events and issues that exist beyond the conventional political agenda. That is where today's global journalist will find the stories that most need to be told.

During the 1990s, those stories were to be found in places such as the Horn of Africa and the Balkans. The values on which foreign policy and international news coverage were based, and the public's attitude toward those values, would be tested as the United States determined what to do about distant wars that, thanks in part to news coverage, could not be ignored.

CHAPTER THREE

⁂

Passion and Dispassion

There is no war without brutality, and those who feel war's harshest pain are often those who are not the combatants, but rather the men, women, and children who may not even understand what the fighting is about. They are innocents who are trapped in a combat zone or who endure the disruptions of life that are the ripple effects of war.

Beyond the human misery inflicted by war are the political ramifications—the damage done to the always fragile international order. Disarray can spread, pulling neighbor after neighbor into a dispute and turning a localized conflict into a regional one, which then can threaten to spread still farther. Like a contagious disease, war may become epidemic if it is not firmly contained.

These are among the reasons for intervention by those who are strong enough to save lives and restore peace. But those with such power may not care to spend their nation's lives and treasure to clean up someone else's mess. If their own security interests are not directly threatened and if their own citizens are not demanding action, why should countries wade into what could prove to be a costly misadventure?

That question is at the heart of a new, soft isolationism that does not absolutely block intervention but does require that an exceptionally compelling case be made before action is undertaken. News coverage often is an integral element of such a case. Depictions of horror in words and pictures and sounds can highlight moral issues that transcend the political strictures that limit responsiveness. If policymakers

39

or the public determine that their security interests encompass more than self-preservation and include preservation of a moral order, then the decision may be made to respond—sometimes with a furious display of power—to a faraway cry for help.

But that doesn't always happen. The journalists who cover the world's wars are sometimes frustrated by what they believe to be the unresponsiveness of governments and the public to the stories they tell and to the events behind them. The wars in Somalia and the former Yugoslavia during the 1990s present striking examples of the interplay between news coverage and policy. Is news coverage a significant factor in the policymaking about such conflicts? The answer is an unequivocal "Perhaps." The impact of news stories is determined first of all by news organizations' own decisions about how much coverage they will present, how thorough it will be, and what, if any, spin is put on stories in terms of emphasizing a particular point of view.

The wars examined in this chapter illustrate the challenges and responsibilities facing journalists who cover such events. Of particular concern is the level of journalists' personal involvement and the extent to which correspondents' personal views should be reflected in their reporting. There is debate within the profession about objectivity: Is it an immutable principle, or is it an unrealistically rigid standard that sometimes obscures the truth?

Journalists and the public will be profoundly affected by the answers to such questions. The standards used in covering the news will do much to determine the influence of that coverage.

Somalia

Somalia is a desolate place, made worse by the viciousness and corruption of those who have held power and by the helplessness of their victims. The misery of the Somali people is excruciating and persistent.

Somalia in 1992 was in particularly awful condition. Dictator Mohamed Siad Barre, who had come to power in a military coup in 1969, fled in 1991 when rebel groups undermined his control of the army. Food shortages became famine when feudal warfare shattered the country's fragile infrastructure. In the CIA's *World Factbook* entry for Somalia, under "government type" the notation was "none" (which was still the case until a tentative change for the better in late 2000). The plight of the Somalis had gone unnoticed by most of the world as the situation worsened. By August 1992, as many as 1.5 million of the estimated 6 million Somalis were threatened with starvation. Approximately 300,000 Somalis had already died, including about 25 percent of all children under the age of five.[1]

Then the news media began paying attention. In 1991, the *New York Times* and *Washington Post* published 186 stories mentioning Somalia. In 1992, the number was 1,025.[2] More important, television networks dispatched crews to Somalia in 1992, and the pictures they sent into homes in the United States and elsewhere were wrenching enough to capture the public's attention. Although images of war may produce revulsion and a vow to keep out of the fighting, reports about starvation elicit sympathy, perhaps enhanced by the self-conscious guilt of the well fed. If the news coverage comes and goes quickly, the public may just as quickly forget what it has seen. But if news organizations deliver a steady stream of reports—particularly ones featuring children and other innocents—then news consumers may start thinking about what they are seeing and ponder possible remedies.

The news media do not stumble into places such as Somalia by accident. They are nudged by politicians, relief organizations, and others who have an interest in the situation. Steven Livingston and Todd Eachus of George Washington University wrote that "the media generally do not serve as independent agents in the development of issues and concerns. Rather, because news agendas typically reflect the agendas of officials, the media serve as instruments of those officials who are most adept at using news to further their policy goals."[3] In the case of Somalia, coverage suggestions emanated from lower echelons of the Bush administration, the United Nations, and a few members of Congress. Among these was Senator Nancy Kassebaum, who after traveling to Somalia and witnessing the country's continuing disintegration, helped push Somalia onto the congressional agenda.

Such pressures on journalists—sometimes subtle, sometimes not—are part of the news business. Story ideas do not materialize spontaneously. Even if they have germinated in the brain of a reporter, editor, or producer, the seed had to come from somewhere. It may have been sown as an offhand remark at a social occasion, or it may have been planted by overt lobbying. Journalistic independence, much vaunted and protected as stories develop, is not necessarily violated by this kind of stimulus. Sources cultivate journalists just as journalists cultivate sources. If an official of an organization such as the International Committee of the Red

Cross calls reporters to alert them to a hitherto overlooked emergency somewhere, most journalists would not feel that their prerogatives had been infringed upon. They would use the tip to start a preliminary determination about whether to pursue the story.

A source is just that, and a line exists between working to follow up on a tip and being used as a conveyor belt for propaganda, even if benign. Finding that line and staying on the proper side of it can be particularly difficult when the story at hand is about a humanitarian crisis that needs immediate attention and when the relief organization that is pushing the journalist seems to have a monopoly on information. How heavily to rely on any single source is always a difficult decision.

Some stories are hard to sell to the news executives who decide what gets covered. Factors include not only the scope of the disaster and the resulting misery, but also who is involved and where it is occurring. Sanford Ungar, journalist and dean of American University's school of communication, said: "It's a Eurocentric bias. It's part of the old myths, and assumptions that the most important things happening in the world at any given time are the things happening in Europe. . . . There is a subtle racism at work. . . . It has to do with frame of mind, with what's immediate, what's familiar, and who stirs the more immediate compassion."[4] *New York Times* media critic Walter Goodman took an even harder line about the sporadic early coverage from Somalia: "Would the signals have excited journalists more if they had come from somewhere else instead of, yet again, black Africa? Just more pictures of flies on sickly black faces? Charges of racism have been much devalued by overuse, and whatever its other failings network news has a strong record against racial abuse at home and abroad. Yet it is difficult to imagine a million or more white children dying in some part of the world without attracting troops of American reporters and more television pictures, no matter how difficult or dangerous the job."[5]

In the case of Somalia, some news organizations responded to cues from sources, but the coverage was slow to have effect. Media scholar Jonathan Mermin wrote: "In the first half of May [1992], CNN presented the crisis in Somalia in extraordinarily dire terms and explicitly criticized the West for declining to act. Yet the CNN stories had no discernible effect on American policy."[6]

After a while, however, the news stories and political rumblings were noticed in the White House. Speaking after the American intervention had occurred, Secretary of State Lawrence Eagleburger told CNN that "television had a great deal to do with President Bush's decision to go in the first place."[7] Eagleburger also said: "This is a tragedy of massive proportions and, underline this, one that we could do something about. We had to act."[8]

Those are intriguing criteria that Eagleburger laid out. There are lots of tragedies of massive proportions around the world. In virtually all of them, the United States "could do something about" improving the situation. In practice, however, U.S. policymakers are much more selective.

There were also counterpressures, such as the warning from the American ambassador to Kenya, Smith Hempstone. He predicted dangers awaiting American troops: "If you liked Beirut, you'll love Mogadishu. . . . Think once, twice, and three times before you embrace the Somali tar baby."[9]

The pro-intervention arguments and images prevailed. In August 1992, Bush ordered an airlift of food and then approved U.S. military transport for Pakistani troops being sent by the United Nations to protect the distribution of relief supplies. Andrew Natsios, who directed relief efforts for the U.S. Agency for International Development, wrote about an important effect of the airlift: "The U.S. military airlift, we knew, would attract an avalanche of media, which we had been unable to mobilize behind the relief effort however hard we had tried. A military airlift is worth a hundred press conferences."[10]

Four months later, Bush sent American forces to Somalia to assist the relief efforts. This was Operation Restore Hope, which took place under the auspices of a UN resolution approving intervention. Within a few weeks, 24,000 American military personnel and 12,000 troops from other nations occupied Somali cities and towns to open supply routes and protect food distribution.[11]

This military initiative was accompanied by a major deployment of journalists, including television's equivalent of the Joint Chiefs of Staff: network anchors. Jonathan Yardley wrote in the *Washington Post* that "for the honchos of the networks, Somalia provides a perfect opportunity to dress up in khaki and do live stand-up feeds as, in the background, African masses gaze at them in speechless awe. Or bewilderment. Or whatever."[12]

The anchors and their colleagues were in place by the time the American Marines came ashore in Mogadishu. The initial landing was turned into a full-fledged media event, with reporters and photographers arrayed on the beach. This led to public criticism about reporters endangering the troops, even though news organizations had been alerted by the Defense Department about the time and place of the landing and had not been asked to stay away. The Pentagon's view, apparently, was that televised images of American military power would deter potential troublemakers.

The landing was a surreal version of a military operation. Jonathan Yardley noted the anchors' presence and wrote: "It does not seem to have occurred to any of these eminences that if the spectacle in Somalia looked for all the world like something out of a farce, it was precisely because they were on hand to make it so. It was staged for their benefit."[13]

This is part of the gamesmanship that pervades the relationship between those who cover and those who are covered. The Pentagon wanted the worldwide television audience to see inspiring pictures of troops coming ashore, and the way to guarantee that those pictures would be available was to make sure the news media were on hand. The fact that camera lights briefly blinded Marines wearing night-vision goggles was brushed aside, as was the possibility that Somali snipers could have taken advantage of the illuminated landing zone and fired on the American force. Certainly far down the list of Pentagon concerns was the chance that journalists might be shot accidentally because of the confusion on the beach.

As a public relations ploy, the Mogadishu landing was successful in getting the public's attention. At this early stage, Americans strongly supported Bush's decision to intervene. In a poll conducted for the *New York Times* and CBS News immediately after the landing, 81 percent of the respondents said they believed that the United States was "doing the right thing in sending troops to Somalia," and 70 percent said they believed that "sending troops to Somalia is worth the possible loss of American lives, financial costs, and other risks."[14]

But not everyone was applauding. Diplomat and scholar George F. Kennan watched the landing on television and was not moved by the nobility of the enterprise. In his diary he wrote that the intervention was unwise "because it treats only a limited and short-term aspect of what is really a much wider and deeper problem. . . . The fact is that this dreadful situation cannot possibly be put to rights other than by the establishment of a governing power for the entire territory, and a very ruthless, determined one at that."[15]

Kennan also questioned the willingness of Congress and the public to undertake such an extensive, rather than short-term, venture. He wrote: "There can be no question that the reason for this acceptance lies primarily with the exposure of the Somalia situation by the American media; above all, television. The reaction would have been unthinkable without this exposure. The reaction was an emotional one, occasioned by the sight of the suffering of the starving people in question. That this should be felt as adequate reason for our military action does credit, no doubt, to the idealism of the American people and to their ready sympathy for people suffering in another part of the world. But this is an emotional reaction, not a thoughtful or deliberate one."[16] As someone who had seen and participated in almost a century's worth of American diplomacy, Kennan worried that policy—particularly that involving use of the military—was increasingly controlled "by popular emotional impulses, and especially ones provoked by the commercial television industry."[17]

Kennan's reaction underscored the dichotomy concerning media influence. By stimulating idealism and sympathy, the news media bring democratic altruism to bear on the policymaking process. But by evoking an emotional response, news coverage may override the level-headed realism that should be a significant ingredient in public policy.

So which is the better course? Answering that requires grappling with the definition of "better," which in turn necessitates striking a balance between narrowly defined "national interest" and the broader concept of humanitarian responsibility. This involves far more than mere semantics; the essence of the debate concerns the duties of a nation that transcend self-interest.

Philosophers and theologians might have a relatively easy time with this, but political leaders—especially those who are directly accountable to voters—may have great difficulty with some of the ramifications of doing good. Kennan wrote that a successful effort in Somalia was bound to require a commitment requiring at least several years and millions, perhaps billions, of dollars, not to mention loss of life. This might not have been apparent to those watching the network anchors narrate the unopposed landings at Mogadishu, but any competent official in the White House, State Department, or Pentagon knew that what was unfolding was more than a television mini-series. The bloody mess that followed in Somalia did not necessarily prove Kennan right, but it did illustrate that there are no simple rescue missions.

George Bush's motives for intervening in Somalia remain cloudy. In *A World Transformed*, the book about his foreign policy that he authored with his national security adviser Brent Scowcroft, Bush gives Somalia only the slightest mention. There is no discussion about what he thought he could accomplish with what he had hoped would be a short-lived American presence. Perhaps he was thinking fondly about the acclaim he received during the Gulf War and believed he might leave office with another foreign triumph. In any event, when Bush vacated the White House the situation in Somalia was far from resolved and was left to Bill Clinton to deal with.

Clinton had stumbled through the transition period, encountering problems with prospective cabinet appointees and with controversial policy initiatives, such as the one concerning gays in the military. Somalia was an inherited problem that he didn't want, and he clearly didn't know what to do with it. He basically maintained the status quo until the United Nations assumed responsibility for the Somalia mission in May · 1993. Although American troops constituted the most potent element of the UN force, the Clinton administration—and the news media—began treating Somalia as a UN rather than U.S. operation. That meant paying less attention to it.

Public opinion experts Andrew Kohut and Robert Toth examined the impact this had: "The development of public support for the new mission was inhibited by American television screens going virtually blank on Somalia for half a year after the Marines landed. Public interest plummeted from 52 percent who said they followed the issue 'very closely' in January to 16 percent in June. In the fall, when the networks and public attention returned to the story, the nature and danger of the mission were very different and support withered rapidly."[18]

Meanwhile, the United Nations was changing the military mission from a humanitarian project to a broader effort to impose order on the chaos that was Somali politics. Doing so would require disarming the ragtag but vicious private armies of Somali warlords. This was a true combat enterprise, far riskier than protecting distribution of food.

Americans' lack of attention to Somalia ended abruptly on October 4, 1993, when a firefight in Mogadishu left 18 Americans and at least 312 Somalis dead, and hundreds on both sides wounded. This was not the first bloodshed during the Somalia intervention, but it was shocking in its magnitude—the largest number of American casualties in a single combat action since the Vietnam War. Photographs published throughout the world showed a dead American serviceman being dragged by Somalis through the streets. A captured American helicopter pilot was videotaped by Somalis and his frightened face appeared on millions of television screens.

In Washington the battle evoked outrage and demands in Congress for an immediate American withdrawal. The news coverage fueled the debate. For example, *Time*'s cover story headline was "What in the World Are We Doing?" *Newsweek*'s was "Trapped in Somalia." Public opinion shifted. Political analyst William Schneider wrote that a week after the Mogadishu battle, Clinton's handling of Somalia was rated by the public at 59 percent negative and 32 percent positive, even though his ratings on other foreign policy issues remained strong (as evidenced by his 54–25 positive rating for his handling of relations with Russia).[19]

Clinton opposed a headlong departure. After meeting with congressional leaders, he announced on October 7 that all U.S. troops would be out of Somalia by March 31, 1994. As policy was being made, the gruesome video and still images from Mogadishu were seen again and again, sustaining the anger and urgency of the debate and, presumably, exerting some influence on policymakers' decisions.

Public reaction toward the news media also was strong, with much criticism of the decision to use the pictures of the dead soldier. But journalists defended their judgment. The *Toronto Star*'s Paul Watson, who took the photos, said, "I think it is important for the people who elect the politicians, and who should decide where their troops go, to know what happens to them." CNN executive Ed Turner said, "It's fair and proper that [the American people] should understand what this kind of warfare is all about."[20]

William Schneider reported that almost 60 percent of respondents in a CNN–*USA Today* poll said they had seen the photos. Half of them said America should withdraw from Somalia immediately, while only a third of the respondents who had *not* seen the photos favored immediate withdrawal.[21]

An ABC News poll found strong support for quick U.S. withdrawal even if that resulted in more famine.[22] Colin Powell later wrote, "We had been drawn into this place by television images; now we were being repelled by them."[23]

But that overstates the influence of the news reports from Mogadishu. There were more substantive factors—rooted in the policymakers' own domain—behind the shifts in public opinion and administration policy. Writing in the *Washington Post*, Duke University's Peter Feaver and Christopher Gelpi reported that "even after the television reports, there was a reservoir of public support for the operation. If the sight of dead American soldiers somewhat undermined it, it was because the Clinton administration made no effort to frame the casualties as anything other than a disaster in a mission that had drifted dreadfully off course. Had the administration chosen instead to galvanize public opposition to Somali warlord Mohamed Farah Aideed, our research suggests that Americans would have tolerated an expanded effort to catch and punish him."[24]

When political leadership allows an information vacuum to exist, the news media will fill it. Given the public's limited baseline knowledge about foreign affairs generally and situations such as that in Somalia more specifically, even superficial information is likely to have disproportionate influence, whether that information comes from the government or the news media. At a time such as the aftermath of the Mogadishu battle, when the public *is* paying attention, if government officials either do not have a coherent policy position or have one but fail to articulate it, then negative news stories and images will have greater impact.

In this case, the argument that grisly pictures from Mogadishu led directly to the collapse of public support for the intervention is an overstatement of media influence. The Clinton White House failed to support its own policy; the resulting political disarray was largely the administration's fault and should not be ascribed to the news media. There is a lesson here for those who will govern in the future.

Along these lines, Robert Kaplan wrote: "Somalia reminded us of this eternal truth of American overseas involvements: human suffering may sometimes be sufficient to get U.S. troops flown to a place, but the moment they start taking casualties there better be a specific national interest at stake, and one that can be communicated succinctly on television, or else the public will cut and run."[25] The American public will accept the necessity of casualties in a military operation, but only if national leaders have made a solid case for that operation and for its likely success. News coverage merely increases the need for that case to be presented in a convincing manner. When politicians blame the media for undercutting public support, they are really admitting their own failure.

Madeleine Albright, while ambassador to the United Nations, told the Senate Foreign Relations Committee: "Television's ability to bring graphic images of pain and outrage into our living rooms has heightened the pressure both for immediate engagement in areas of international crisis and immediate disengagement when events do not go according to plan. Because we live in a democratic society, none of us can be oblivious to those pressures."[26] The rejoinder to Albright could be "What about leadership?" Granted, policymakers should not be oblivious to public opinion, but they could present a stronger case in support of their position and try to shape public opinion accordingly.

After U.S. forces withdrew in 1994, other UN peacekeepers remained until 1995. The 1997 "Cairo declaration" established a semblance of coalition government that exercised authority in parts of Somalia. The UN/U.S. intervention did undoubtedly save lives by getting some relief supplies to those who desperately needed them, but the root causes of the Somali famine—political chaos and the lack of economic infrastructure—were not remedied. Somalia will probably be a very sad place for a very long time.

Some of the journalists who covered Somalia remain frustrated by the world's lack of interest in the tragic events there, even though the news media delivered at least enough information to let people know generally what was going on. Scott Peterson, who has spent many years covering Africa for several news organizations, wrote: "Is it possible—is it wise?—to remain so uninterested in the fate of our fellow humans? Or is some fast-food strip town in eastern Oklahoma so remote from the outside world that all those creatures *out there* in Africa and elsewhere aren't really in the same 'human' category?"[27]

Having seen the pervasive wretchedness of Somalia, Peterson has reason to be angry about Americans' apparent nonchalance about distant tragedies. In his book about Africa's wars, *Me Against My Brother*, Peterson runs up against the limits of journalistic power. He can tell the story, but it is up to governments and their constituencies to act.

Not only have post–Cold War American presidents failed to create a philosophy on which to base unilateral intervention decisions, but they also have not been consistent when other countries or international organizations such as the United Nations want to take the lead and ask for American support. This has sometimes led to paralysis in the face of humanitarian emergencies. It affects news coverage as well because there is no clear standard that journalists might use in appraising the adequacy of response to those emergencies.

The unhappy American experience in Somalia produced the "Somalia doctrine," an unofficial but nevertheless potent mandate to avoid involvement in distant crises unless a clearly definable American security interest is in jeopardy. That is politically convenient, if morally shabby. It serves as an excuse for the most powerful nation in the world to remain uninvolved.

This doctrine can also obstruct the path between news coverage and the public's conscience. When political leaders are predisposed to oppose humanitarian intervention, news consumers may pay less attention to stories about the situations where such intervention might be needed. Compassion needs to be nurtured not only by the news media but also by those whose job is to lead. Absent such moral leadership, the impact of news coverage will be limited.

Bosnia

The fracturing of what had been Yugoslavia was a function of the altered post–Cold War power structure. Had a robust Soviet Union still existed, independence movements would almost certainly have been squelched in Slovenia, Croatia, and elsewhere. Absent that inhibiting menace or any other effective barrier, varied nationalist politics gained traction and Yugoslavia began to break apart.

Western parochialism ensures that conflict in Europe will always receive prompt attention, even if not prompt action. Warfare in modern Europe is viewed as unseemly by the political hierarchy. The protagonists are at least vaguely "like us," and their disarray reflects badly on the established order. The machinery of diplomacy rattles, wheezes, and sputters as the UN, NATO, and ad hoc peacemakers try to respond. The public—unless tied to the unpleasantness by historic kinship or by having to deal with a stream of refugees—pays less attention, at least at first.

Stopping armed conflict is the business of governments and other political institutions, but they are not very good at it, as the worsening situation in the Balkans proved. Ivo Daalder, who was the National Security Council's director for European affairs in 1995 and 1996, wrote: "The collective failure of these regional and international institutions to deal with Yugoslavia's disintegration was due to many factors, including institutional incompetence and overconfidence. But at bottom, it was a failure of the major powers, which used the institutions in an attempt to obfuscate their own unwillingness to employ the right combination of diplomacy and force to end the fighting. In the end, it was a failure of the United States, first in deferring to the Europeans while failing to back them up, and then in trying to intervene with half-measures designed more to limit risks than to have an impact on the ground."[28]

That indictment is sweeping but accurate. A failure of will or a failure of competence is certain to undermine even good intentions. During the early months of the Clinton administration, U.S. officials clearly did not know how to respond. Secretary of State Warren Christopher referred to the fighting in Bosnia as "a confusing, horrific three-way war."[29] Colin Powell wrote: "The meetings we held on Bosnia were full of belligerent rhetoric. But what aggressive action were we to take, and to what end?"[30] Even when officials did have something to say, their pronouncements meant little. Journalist Nik Gowing found that "sound-bites and declarations of horror or condemnation were usually misread in TV and newspaper reporting as signals of hardening of policy—which they were not. They were what one official described to me as often 'pseudo-decisions for pseudo-action.'"[31]

While those with the power to affect the war spun their wheels, the fighting continued and the level of suffering increased. The slow pace at which policymakers moved could be attributed to wise caution, or it could have been a function of the absence of political resolve to do more and do it faster. At such times, news coverage might help move the process along. Journalist Warren Strobel wrote in 1994 that "Bosnia fits neatly into what might be called the First Law of Media Effects: The news media's capacity to influence is inversely related to the degree of consensus in government and society. . . . In Bosnia, on the frequent occasions when U.S. policy was in flux and there was still a chance of military intervention, the news media's words and pictures could give the system a shudder."[32]

In Bosnia itself, meanwhile, news coverage—particularly by television—was valued by those humanitarian organizations trying to alleviate the suffering of the war's victims. Sylvana Foa, spokesperson for the UN's High Commission for Refugees, said: "Without TV coverage we are nothing. Our operations and their impact would die without TV."[33] Nevertheless, there was also bitter irony about the limited effect news coverage was having. One Bosnian Muslim told Peter Maass of the *Washington Post:* "We can watch CNN. We can watch reports about our own genocide!"[34]

Even when they heard such comments and were caught up in the day-to-day horrors of the fighting, many reporters made it a point to remain emotionally outside the story they were covering. Maass wrote: "Journalists observe other people's tragedies; we rarely experience them. The difference is immense."[35] *Newsday*'s Roy Gutman said: "Your number one concern on earth is getting the full story, getting out of there, and getting the story out. You don't have time for emotions. You really just simply concentrate on what you're doing."[36]

Despite this formal detachment, many correspondents became increasingly frustrated by the world's lack of response to the war. Martin Bell was asked by Bosnians about the world's reaction. "I could hardly answer," he wrote, "that it was none of my business. It was everybody's business, even that of the journalists passing by: perhaps *especially* that of the journalists, because if the world didn't know, its ignorance was our failure."[37]

David Rieff, a veteran member of the press corps covering Bosnia, knew that some of the correspondents there thought it was an important part of their job to get the world's attention, win its sympathy, and provoke a useful response. "All along," he wrote, "it had been the task many of the journalists set themselves, consciously or unconsciously, to change the sentiments of their readers and viewers about the slaughter. That was why, throughout the siege [of Sarajevo], the reporters and television crews were perhaps the only dependable allies the Bosnians had. The Bosnian government, which had bet everything on foreign intervention, understood the influence of the press corps early on."[38] Perhaps *thought* they understood would be more accurate. People desperately seeking hope may overrate the news media's clout.

Rieff also understood that journalists themselves sometimes overestimated the effects of their reporting. "It was the conceit of journalists," he wrote, "that if people back home could only be told and shown what was actually happening in Sarajevo, if they had to see on their television screens images of what a child who has just been hit by a soft-nosed bullet or a jagged splinter of shrapnel really looks like, or the bodies of citizens massacred as they queued for bread or water, then they would want their governments to do something. The hope of the Western press was that an informed citizenry back home would demand that their governments not allow the Bosnian Muslims to go on being massacred, raped, or forced from their homes."[39]

That proved to be wishful thinking. In some cases, reporters' frustration became manifest in a more aggressive journalism that its champions considered morally essential. This reporting described the abundant evil and identified its perpetrators. Christiane Amanpour of CNN was among these. She told an interviewer that "an element of morality has to be woven into these kinds of stories. I don't think it has anything to do with an agenda. Simply it has everything to do with what is going on in front of your eyes. Governments, particularly in the West, were telling their versions of the truth about Bosnia. If we had blindly repeated that in the name of so-called objectivity, and not said, 'But hang on; in fact, this is what we know is going on,' then we would be giving eternal life to the lies."[40] Further challenging the sanctity of "objectivity," Amanpour asked: "What does that word mean? I have come to believe that objectivity means giving all sides a fair hearing, but not treating all sides equally. Once you treat all sides the same in a case such as Bosnia, you are drawing a moral equivalence between victim and aggressor. And from there it is a short step toward being neutral. And from there it's an even shorter step to becoming an accessory to all manners of evil; in Bosnia's case, genocide. So objectivity must go hand in hand with morality."[41]

Amanpour also said: "With this war, it was not possible for a human being to be neutral. Life obviously is full of gray areas most of the time. But sometimes in life, there are clear examples of black and white."[42] On another occasion, Amanpour said, "When you are neutral, you can become an accomplice and in these kinds of situations you are an accomplice to the most unspeakable crimes against humanity."[43]

Similarly, David Rieff wrote: "It is said that the press corps became too involved with what was going on in Bosnia, that it should have remained more dispassionate. There is some truth to this. It is hard to be dispassionate about ethnic cleansing and mass murder."[44]

Amanpour was even willing to battle the president of the United States. In a CNN "Global Forum" in 1994, with Bill Clinton in an American studio and Amanpour on a Sarajevo street, the reporter challenged the president: "As leader of the free world, as leader of the only superpower, why has it taken you, the United States, so long to articulate a policy on Bosnia? Why, in the absence of a policy, have you allowed the U.S. and the West to be held hostage to those who do have a clear policy, the Bosnian Serbs?" She then criticized Clinton for "the constant flip-flop of your administration on the issue of Bosnia." The visibly angry Clinton responded, "There have been no constant flip-flops, madam."[45]

Policymakers took note of Amanpour's forceful on-air presence. One senior U.S. official said that Amanpour had become a symbol of "the evil press that undermines military policy and creates political pressures that can't be dealt with rationally. . . . She is a particular obsession with the military. We routinely sit around and try to figure out how to react when she shows up at the scene of some tragedy." Amanpour's response was: "If governments don't like what we are doing, that is their problem. We will be there to cover as much as we can. If they try to bar us, we will try to find ways of showing what is going on."[46]

The advocacy of Amanpour and some other journalists might be considered a triumph of conscience over unduly rigid standards for news gathering. Although objectivity is considered by many to be fundamental to ethical journalism, Amanpour has argued that there is a higher ethical duty, in this case to the Bosnian Muslims being victimized by the Serbs. David Rieff underscored this point of view, saying that "to be fair and to be impartial are not the same thing."[47]

This is more than a question of semantics, and it affects more than the content of any given news report. It goes to the heart of the relationship between the news media and public. Fairness and impartiality might not be the same thing, but absent impartiality, will coverage still be perceived as fair by news consumers? With much of the public already skeptical about the news media's practices and intentions, any modification of the standard of objectivity should be undertaken with great care.

Even if the Bosnian Muslims, as victims of Serb atrocities, should be depicted sympathetically, a case can be made that this can be done by reporting the facts dispassionately, without journalists appointing themselves advocates for the Muslim position. David Binder of the *New York Times* said, "Our job is to report from all sides, not to play favorites."[48] John Buckley of Christian Science Monitor Radio said that "if you allow yourself to demonize one side in a dispute, then you lose credibility."[49]

Martin Bell noted that the international press corps in Sarajevo "soon came to be on the side of the Muslims, not only geographically but also morally. Indifference was not an option open to us. Some reporters' sympathies were co-opted so openly that they started to refer to the Serbs, in the language of the Bosnian presidency, as 'aggressor forces.' The Serbs' case, even if they had one, went unheard."[50] But Bell himself noted a substantive flaw in the resulting coverage: "I would ask myself, when had we ever shown a civilian victim of sniper fire on the Serb side of the lines? When had we reported from their hospitals?"[51]

Correspondents on the scene were not the only ones to editorialize. A 1994 ABC News special, "While America Watched: The Bosnia Tragedy," drew praise from *Washington Post* media critic Tom Shales as being "the kind of thing a network news division ought to be doing just for the sake of doing it." Shales noted that "the broadcast has a strong point of view. At least five times [ABC anchor Peter] Jennings accuses the United States of 'standing by' while the Serbs have rained havoc down on Muslims and Croats."[52] A year later, *New York Times* media critic Walter Goodman wrote: "Possibly out of disappointment at its failure to rouse Americans to demand action, network news has turned up the heat on the White House. On NBC, the relatively restrained Tom Brokaw said, 'Another no-win for the White House: the nightmare scenario in Bosnia.' The lead-ins by Mr. Jennings [on ABC], who has done strong reports of his own from Bosnia, have been particularly pointed: 'Once again Bosnian civilians forced to flee their homes in terror while the Western European nations and the United States do nothing about it.'"[53]

Recognizing that some reporters were sympathetic to their cause, Bosnian Muslim officials, wrote Martin Bell, would provoke the Serbs to incur retaliation. "And where the shells landed and did their indiscriminate damage, the cameras would never be far away. Nor would the [Bosnian] government spokesmen demanding action. This was the way that wars were waged in the age of satellite television and UN peace enforcement: a military victory could also be a political defeat. The Muslims could win the war by losing it. And vice versa the Serbs."[54]

Personal conscience and manipulation by the protagonists may tug at journalists as they cover stories such as the fighting in Bosnia. In such circumstances, it is easy to drift away from objectivity. But at the heart of the journalist's job is the need to find a balance between delivery of narrowly defined "news" and thoughtful presentation of the broader truth. The latter involves providing interpretation of events and conveying nuance, which can be done without crossing into advocacy.

Several cases during this war illustrate the pressures on journalists and how they might respond.

The Camps

Newsday reporter Roy Gutman received the call on July 9, 1992. A Muslim political leader in Banja Luka, Bosnia's second-largest city, urged Gutman to come quickly: "There is a lot of killing. They are shipping Muslim people through Banja Luka in cattle cars. Last night there were twenty-five train wagons for cattle crowded with women, old people, and children. They were so frightened. You could see their hands through the openings. We were not allowed to come close. Can you imagine that? It's like Jews being sent to Auschwitz. In the name of humanity, please come."[55]

Gutman went. He was able to confirm that the deportations had occurred, and he found leads to two other major stories: mass murder in Serb-run concentration camps, and systematic rape by Serb troops. In a lengthy series of articles for *Newsday*, Gutman detailed the savagery he uncovered. The first story, headlined "Death Camps: Survivors Tell of Captivity, Mass Slaughters in Bosnia," got the attention of governments and other news organizations. His work won the Pulitzer Prize and many other awards.

More important, Gutman's stories had effect, most significantly within the usually impervious Serbian government. He later wrote: "In a small country like Serbia that ultimately wants recognition, publicity can make a difference. Within a day or so of *Newsday*'s report on death camps, the Bosnian Serbs closed Omarska, one of the biggest camps, dispersed the prisoners, and opened the facility to news media and the International Red Cross."[56] This was a small triumph—atrocities continued elsewhere in the war zone—but the press-generated pressure resulted in at least some alleviation of misery.

There was, however, little substantive response from governments. Secretary of State Warren Christopher said that events in Bosnia constituted merely "a humanitarian crisis a long way from home, in the middle of another continent," and added that "our actions are proportionate to what our responsibilities are. We can't do it all."[57]

Policy decisions about how much a government can and will do are only occasionally based on information drawn from news coverage. Many political issues come into play. Officials consult the polls and their political gurus. They ponder how their actions on one issue will affect other matters. Somewhere along the line, conscience may assert itself, but it may be quickly dismissed as unsettling and inconvenient. It is locked away until the political mood changes. Then it is rediscovered with great flourish and paraded for all the world to admire.

Journalists should not be deterred by the often insensitive reaction to their reporting. They have to find the story and tell it. Gutman said: "Somewhere, back in my first thoughts about going into journalism, I considered that maybe if reporters had been out there to issue warnings at the time [about the Holocaust], they could have stopped it. And maybe that's the way to stop the killing in Bosnia now. . . . We can't watch passively while people are being killed in front of us. There are higher requirements. As a reporter, you can't simply sit there and report passively. You've got to do everything in your power to stop these things, and exposing it is one of the best ways to do it."[58]

Gutman also said: "We can only do so much. We cannot stop wars or even, regrettably, halt the killing of innocents. But, with careful work, we can alert the public to what is happening in the hopes that the public will react. It's difficult if you're up against the complacency of people with other things to worry about and the apathy of major governments, but it's worth a try to tell people what may be at stake. They have to make the decision."[59]

Reading Gutman's articles, one is struck by the absence of the sensational trappings that some reporters would have added to such horrific stories. The *Newsday* pieces (which are collected in his book, *A Witness to Genocide*) are solid reporting. Whenever possible, he has first-person testimony from victims, corroboration, and comments from Serb officials. Gutman told an interviewer that "unlike many of my colleagues, I did spend more time with the Serbs, reporting them and watching them, rather than spending time with the victims in Sarajevo who were being shot at from a long distance. I wanted to get inside the machine, and I made a lot of effort to do that. If you weren't in the thick of it where they actually were doing the [ethnic] cleansing and running the camps, you could hardly discern the truth. When I could see how clear it was, it drove me on."[60]

Gutman did not explicitly make a case against the Serbs. He let the facts in his stories do that. He said, "I've always felt that the best journalism was not advocacy journalism but simply the straightforward reporting of extraordinary information that reflects unacceptable practices or behavior." That should lead to action, but it often doesn't. He said in an interview: "This will be recorded as the first genocide in history where journalists were reporting it as it was actually happening and governments didn't stop it. It's outrageous and hypocritical."[61]

If Gutman had been more dramatic or more partisan in his storytelling, would that have made a difference? Probably not. Gutman, like any realistic journalist, knows that "the power of the press" has clear limits. Tell the story well and hope for the best. When the best doesn't happen, tell the story again. As chapter four illustrates, Bosnia may have been the first but it was certainly not the last place where the world watched war crimes being committed without adequately responding.

The Sarajevo Market

It was Saturday, February 5, 1994, just past noon–a nice day with a sunny touch of early spring that offered respite from the tensions of war. It was a peaceful day, not one of those punctuated by explosions. The outdoor market in the center of downtown Sarajevo, close by the Catholic cathedral, was crowded with shoppers.

In an instant, 68 of them were killed and approximately 200 wounded when a mortar shell lobbed from somewhere on the city's perimeter exploded into the market. The scene resembled a slaughterhouse–blood everywhere and human limbs scattered about. Television crews were quickly on the scene, many of them arriving before the dead and wounded had been carried away. Within a short time the world could see the carnage.

In the aftermath of this incident, Western policy toward the Serbs changed. The television coverage did not, in itself, shape those changes. Nik Gowing pointed out that "it was the massacre itself, not the TV images, that catalyzed a diplomatic process that had been underway for several weeks."[62] The policy change incorporated the basics of an earlier French proposal and involved establishing an "exclusion zone" around Sarajevo. The Serbs were required to remove their heavy weapons from the area or place them under UN control. Further shelling of Sarajevo would be met by NATO air strikes on Serb positions.

This is not to say that the news reports did not matter. In her book about the first year-and-a-half of the Clinton presidency, Elizabeth Drew wrote: "Whether the administration and its allies would have done anything militarily about Sarajevo if the attack, and the terrible television pictures, had not happened cannot be known. The administration had been moving toward a new policy of diplomacy that could have used military force, but this hadn't involved setting up the special protection for Sarajevo. And there's a strong question as to whether NATO would have agreed to any new policy absent the mortar attack."[63]

The whole policy continuum during years of fighting in various parts of the former Yugoslavia deserves critical analysis. Much of the diplomacy was poorly conceived and ineffectual. The news media's performance deserves similar analysis. Like Western policy, the news coverage had its ups and downs, peaking (in terms of amount of coverage) during moments of the most sensational outrages, while offering much less consistent reporting at other times. After the Sarajevo market attack, an editor of one of that city's newspapers, *Oslobodenje*, asked, "Why is there all this fuss in the West about one incident?"[64] Events such as the market shelling were not uncommon, in Sarajevo and elsewhere, but rarely received international television coverage. When an even more destructive shelling occurred in Tuzla in 1995, it received little notice because the television coverage was limited.

Despite inconsistencies in long-term coverage, the reports from the Sarajevo market may have had political effect that rippled into policymaking. R. W. Apple of the *New York Times* wrote: "The frightful television images of the carnage may have broken, or at least dented, the shell of American public indifference. At the least, they have given the President as good an opportunity to act firmly in Bosnia as he is likely to get."[65] Also in the *New York Times*, Walter Goodman wrote: "So, is the apparent stiffening of Washington's attitude something positive: an example of a resistant Administration being compelled to act by the nation's conscience, newly jolted by terrible pictures? Or is it negative: an example of officials being coerced to adjust their policies to the moment's surge of emotion generated by television?"[66]

Assuming Clinton had the inclination to act, the video from Sarajevo may have bolstered public opinion in a way that made his doing so politically easier. But a Gallup poll following the market attack found only a 48 percent to 43 percent margin in favor of air strikes, so whatever help the news reports generated was far from overwhelming.[67] In *Newsweek*, Michael Elliott wrote: "Start with the obvious–that there has been little public demand in either Europe or America for military intervention. This, unnoticed, has blasted a piece of late twentieth century conventional wisdom. Remember the global village? Time was when it was thought that the instant transmission of television pictures of horror would provoke an outcry that the world must 'do something' to make the horror cease. Not in the case of Bosnia."[68]

The Sarajevo attack illustrates one of the effects of news coverage in such situations, at least from the policymakers' standpoint: it may create political cover for politicians who are reluctant to lead. Journalists recognize the difference between passive and active policy, and they understand how news reports can occasionally serve as a bridge from the former to the latter. To overestimate the potency of coverage, however, would be a mistake. The components of a substantive policy initiative are unlikely to be altered by the way the news media treat an event. For their part, journalists should be wary about overestimating their own clout and should not succumb to any temptation to hype a story with an eye to affecting policy.

Srebrenica

Nestled in an eastern corner of Bosnia-Herzegovina, near the border with Serbia, Srebrenica was perpetually vulnerable. It was easily targeted by Serb artillery and could be quickly blockaded to keep out supply convoys. The persistent misery of its residents received only sporadic news coverage, partly because it was often impossible for reporters to reach.

A Serb artillery attack on April 12, 1993, killed fifty-six Srebrenica residents, including children who had been playing on a soccer field. The scene was described by an official working for the UN High Commissioner for Refugees (UNHCR): "Fourteen dead bodies were found in the schoolyard. Body parts and human flesh clung to the schoolyard fence. The ground was literally soaked with blood. One child, about six years of age, had been decapitated. I saw two ox carts covered with bodies. I did not look forward to closing my eyes at night for fear that I would relive the images. I will never be able to convey the horror." Another UNHCR official on the scene said: "My first thought was for the commander who gave the order to attack. I hope he burns in the hottest corner of hell."[69]

On March 12, 1993, French general Philippe Morillon, the commander of UN forces in Bosnia, promised residents of Srebrenica: "You are now under the protection of the United Nations. I will never abandon you."[70] This made him a hero in Srebrenica but angered his superiors, who were not in the business of promising to "never abandon" anyone.

The following month, Srebrenica surrendered to the Serbs. The United Nations Protective Force (UNPROFOR) quickly engineered a post facto "ceasefire," a term UN officials insisted on using rather than "surrender." A small, lightly armed force of peacekeepers was left in Srebrenica, but two years later the United Nations was gone, the Serbs were in control, and 7,000 Muslim men from the town were missing.

Even the minimal and temporary UN presence occurred partly because news reports by ABC's Tony Birtley and others alerted the world to the misery of Srebrenica's civilian residents. By 1995, the Serbs had effectively blocked press access to the town. Their conquest of Srebrenica and their vengeance on the Bosnian Muslims there were later documented by David Rohde of the *Christian Science Monitor* and others. The story is excruciating, not only as a recounting of the atrocities inflicted, but also as a portrait of negligence on the part of the United Nations and the Western powers. In his book *Endgame*, Rohde wrote: "What occurred in Srebrenica was unprecedented in postwar

Europe. Srebrenica is unique because of the international community's role in the tragedy. The international community partially disarmed thousands of men, promised them they would be safeguarded and then delivered them to their sworn enemies. Srebrenica was not simply a case of the international community standing by as a far-off atrocity was committed. The actions of the international community encouraged, aided, and emboldened the executioners."[71]

While governments dithered, press criticism mounted. In *The New Republic,* Charles Lane wrote: "The assessment of UN officials and Western governments is that Srebrenica was militarily indefensible—that there was no way to prevent the enclave, hemmed in by Serb-held high ground, from falling. This is about half true. Srebrenica was militarily indefensible—but only because the UN military deterrent operated under ambiguous and unwieldy rules designed less to protect Bosnians than to avoid Western casualties and obscure the accountability of Western governments."[72]

Charles Trueheart wrote in the *Washington Post* that "on at least one count—the abundance of blame and shame on all sides—the Bosnia impasse has provoked an unusual unanimity on the editorial and opinion pages in Paris, London, and Washington." As an example, he cited Andrew Neil in the *Sunday Times* of London, who wrote about President Clinton: "All he had to say was that the fall of Srebrenica had undermined the UN's peacekeeping mission in Bosnia. But we do not need presidents to state the obvious; the shaming of the UN and the humiliation of NATO, which provides its firepower, were there for all to see."[73]

Srebrenica consistently vexed American policymakers. After the 1993 surrender of the town, Clinton said, "The U.S. should always seek an opportunity to stand up against—at least speak out against—inhumanity." That was a carefully ambiguous statement, and Elizabeth Drew noted that "there was quite a disparity within that one sentence."[74] Speaking out occurred rarely enough, but Clinton's words implied that this would be as far as the United States would go. Actually standing up against inhumanity was just too much to expect.

In 1995, after seeing a story and photograph in the *Washington Post* of a despondent young woman refugee from Srebrenica who had hanged herself, Vice President Al Gore said in an Oval Office meeting: "The worst solution would be to acquiesce to genocide and allow the rape of another city and more refugees. At the same time we can't be driven by images because there's plenty of other places that aren't being photographed where terrible things are going on. But we can't ignore the images either."[75] That, too, neatly avoids defining a policy position, but it indicates that even belated news coverage was getting officials' attention.

Later in 1995, David Rohde received a tip from an intelligence agency official that aerial reconnaissance photos suggested the existence of mass graves near Srebrenica. He traveled to the area and found compelling evidence before being arrested by the Serbs. (The Clinton administration later pressured the Serbs to release him.)[76] Such evidence led Assistant Secretary of State Richard Holbrooke to describe the events in Srebrenica as "a war crime of major proportions." He said the fall of the town was a "historic event" that inspired Western governments to block Serb military advances and more assertively seek a negotiated end to the war.[77]

Although the story of Srebrenica may have given diplomats a needed jolt, its telling was not an unalloyed triumph of journalism. Because of the town's inaccessibility, reports were delayed and incomplete. And even those journalists who anticipated the tragedy could do little before it happened. The BBC's Allan Little said, "We failed because we weren't clear enough about what was going on because we were frightened by the big stick of balance and objectivity and neutrality."[78]

Nevertheless, even when reporters are not immediately at the scene, their role is important. What if correspondents such as David Rohde had not pursued the story even when it was "old news"? Those residents of Srebrenica who were "missing" might never have had a claim on the world's conscience. The news stories about them and their town became their inadequate but still important legacy.

Effects on Policy and Public

One of the ways that news reports affect policymakers is by providing information that may not be available—at least not as promptly—from diplomats, intelligence agencies, and other official sources. Smaller nations that do not have their own information-gathering mechanisms may rely more heavily on news coverage. Although these countries do not have much clout on their own, their stance in multinational bodies such as the United Nations may be influenced by what they see in the news media.

The major powers are affected most by news coverage in a political context, as policymakers gauge how the public is responding to news stories. Most officials at least claim to resist news-based demands for policy shifts. During the fighting in Bosnia, British foreign secretary Douglas Hurd said, "We have not been and are not willing to begin some form of military intervention which we judge useless or worse simply because of day by day pressures from the media."[79]

In 1993, during the early months of the Clinton presidency, joint chiefs chairman General Colin Powell adopted much the same position as Hurd took. But news coverage can intensify debate even within the highest echelons of the government. Powell found himself challenged by UN ambassador Madeleine Albright, who during a White House meeting asked him, "What's the point of having this superb military that you're always talking about if we can't use it?" Powell wrote: "I thought I would have an aneurysm. American GIs were not toy soldiers to be moved around on some sort of global game board."[80] The Albright-Powell disagreement may well have occurred even if there had been no media-related pressures, but news coverage can add urgency to policy discussions. When lives are being lost, as was the case in Bosnia, the slow-moving policy process might benefit from being pushed along.

The public may have been shocked and even outraged by some of the news reports from Bosnia, but those reactions tended to be transient. Surveys in late 1994 found that despite reports about atrocities and "considerable news sentiment in favor of helping the Bosnians," only 30 percent of respondents said the United States had a responsibility to act, while 62 percent said it did not.[81]

Writing about this in 1995 in the *New York Times*, Walter Goodman commented: "More than three years of scenes of atrocities may not have enhanced Serbia's reputation in the United States, but the response around the country has been notable mainly for its lack of passion. There has been no surge of demands on the White House to do something, which may account in part for its hesitancy."[82] In the *Los Angeles Times* in 1995, Howard Rosenberg asked, "Have we, the U.S. public, watching all of this securely from across the sea, gotten so used to these now-nightly pictures of violence and sorrowful victims that they've become abstractions?"[83] Rosenberg's concern was similar to that expressed by Warren Strobel in the *Christian Science Monitor*: "If TV did have an impact in Bosnia, I suspect it was a more subtle and perhaps more dangerous one: to add to the viewer's frustration and cynicism about the ability of his or her government to do anything about the world's seemingly unsolvable and ever-present problems."[84]

Given this apparent absence of Americans' willingness to act, journalists may wonder if their arduous and often dangerous work is worth doing. For many reporters, being discouraged is understandable, especially in light of their own reaction to the horrors they have seen. But change in public opinion is almost always incremental, and journalists must hope that their reporting is chipping away at insensitivity. That may be a fragile rationale for proceeding, but if the correspondents who covered the former Yugoslavia had not been there to report what was happening, the resolve of the West may have been even shakier, the atrocities even worse, and perhaps Slobodan Milosevic's presidency would have survived, instead of falling in October 2000. Even within Serbia, there were those who remembered what the press had reported about their own leaders' actions. As part of a larger process, news coverage does matter.

According to NATO secretary-general Lord Robertson, by the time the 1995 Dayton Accords were signed, 200,000 people had died during three-and-a-half years of fighting in Bosnia and Herzegovina. Two million people had been driven from their homes. Industrial production had fallen to 5 percent of prewar levels. Eighty percent of the population was totally dependent on outside aid.[85]

For forty-two months, the world had watched this. Neither governments nor–in most of the world–the general public could claim that they had not been told what was going on. The news media had done their job. Sometimes the reporting was belated or incomplete, sometimes it was simplistic or sensationalized, but much of the coverage was solid and conveyed the essence of the conflict to anyone who chose to pay attention.

As the debate within this chapter illustrates, the question for news professionals covering misery such as existed in Bosnia, Somalia, and many other places is not so much about reportorial competence as it is about the moral boundaries of journalism. How far should journalists go in making judgments about good and evil? Should passion about events be supplied only by the news audience rather than the news providers? How can the human beings who gather the news remain "objective" in the face of the horrors they cover? What are journalists' responsibilities when they discover concentration camps or mass graves or hear the stories of women who have been raped or children who are starving?

Finding answers to such questions becomes more difficult and more important when the international community fails to respond adequately to a major humanitarian crisis. In Somalia and Bosnia, governments did act, even if neither promptly nor comprehensively. In Rwanda in 1994, as hundreds of thousands of people were being killed, the international community did little more than talk until it was too late for action.

At a time when laissez-faire foreign policy is convenient and popular, interventionism has little support, even when a truly horrific situation occurs. Particularly when events move quickly, as was the case in Rwanda, the speed and substance of the rest of the world's response are often inadequate.

The news media are also tested in these situations. Can they tell the story thoroughly and clearly enough to capture the world's attention and perhaps help accelerate a response? Rwanda presented just such a test.

CHAPTER FOUR

Witness

Even when news stories are timely, accurate, and get the world's attention, there is no guarantee that governments will respond. For the correspondents in the midst of events, this can be excruciating. They see terrible things happening that they know could be stopped if only those with power would muster the will to do so.

In these situations, the journalists are witnesses who tell their stories to all who will listen. But that is not always enough. They want to see justice arrive. Sometimes it finally does.

The 1994 Rwanda war was a staggering example of vast, pervasive evil. At first, news organizations and governments resisted labeling the slaughter as genocide, but that is what it was. The public's response was also sluggish, matching the pace and tone of the news coverage.

Whose fault was this? In the aftermath of the Rwanda killing, with so many dead, it is natural to want to fix blame for the lack of response. There is certainly enough fault and shame to be shared by many, including the news media. But as this chapter illustrates, journalists did their job—not as well as it should have been done, but well enough to lift the fog of disbelief and alert the world to what was happening.

There were, however, major flaws not just in reporting about Rwanda, but in Western news organizations' coverage of Africa generally. Although rarely admitted, race affects news priorities, and it affects governments' decisions about whether to intervene in a conflict.

For the individual journalist who witnesses crimes against humanity, detachment may be superseded by personal commitment to helping justice prevail. How involved the journalist ought to be in this process should be considered carefully.

The global journalist will witness many of civilization's most ghastly failings. This chapter looks at how that journalist might best respond.

Rwanda

Encompassing slightly more than 10,000 square miles, Rwanda is one of the world's smallest countries. It is also the most densely populated nation in Africa. It has rich soil and receives ample rain, and so is capable of feeding itself and producing coffee for export. Rwanda could thrive, but in recent decades it has been more intent on tearing itself apart. In the early 1990s, roughly 85 percent of the country's population were Hutus and about 15 percent were Tutsis. Beginning in 1959, there had been periodic fighting between them, reaching its peak in 1994.

On April 6, 1994, Rwandan president Juvenal Habyarimana was killed when his plane was apparently shot down by unknown parties on the ground in Kigali, Rwanda's capital. Habyarimana was a Hutu who had been inching toward implementing an arrangement for sharing power with the Tutsis, as prescribed by the Arusha Peace Accord of 1993. This may have led to his being murdered by extremist Hutus. Whatever the reason for his death, Rwanda's Tutsis immediately found themselves targets of an effort to eliminate them.

Within hours of Habyarimana's death, the Rwandan army and Hutu militias set up roadblocks where they checked identity papers. When they found Tutsis, they killed them. The Hutu forces also went from house to house, murdering Tutsis and moderate Hutus. Their thoroughness was evidence of a carefully planned mass murder campaign. The state radio station, Radio Mille Collines, fed the murderous hatred, urging Hutus to defend Rwanda against Tutsi "inyenzi" (cockroaches) and to fill the country's rivers with Tutsi dead.

UN peacekeeping troops in the country (UNAMIR: United Nations Assistance Mission for Rwanda) had neither the mandate nor the strength to intervene. Ten Belgian UN soldiers assigned to protect the moderate Hutu prime minister were captured by the Hutu forces, who then killed the prime minister and the Belgians. A week later, Belgium withdrew from the UN operation. In another incident, UN soldiers who had been protecting 2,000 refugees at a school were ordered to withdraw to the airport, leaving the refugees behind. Most of these civilians were then killed.

A week after Belgium withdrew, the UN Security Council voted unanimously to pull out most of the remaining troops, reducing the UNAMIR presence from 2,500 to 270. The killing continued. Canadian general Romeo Dallaire, commander of UNAMIR, lamented his inability to respond to the murder around him, writing that "my force was standing knee-deep in mutilated bodies, surrounded by the guttural moans of dying people, looking into the eyes of children bleeding to death with their wounds burning in the sun and being invaded by maggots and flies."[1]

No precise count can ever be made, but reasonable estimates of the number killed range from 600,000 to 1.2 million. Most of them died during just 100 days in a low-tech frenzy that featured the machete as its principal weapon. (By comparison, the death toll in the four-year war among Serbs, Croats, and Bosnian Muslims in the former Yugoslavia was about 200,000.)

In his book *We Wish to Inform You That Tomorrow We Will Be Killed with Our Families*, Philip Gourevitch describes the process: "Hutus young and old rose to the task. Neighbors hacked neighbors to death in their homes, and colleagues hacked colleagues to death in their workplaces. Doctors killed their patients, and schoolteachers killed their pupils. Within days, the Tutsi populations of many villages were all but eliminated, and in Kigali prisoners were released in work gangs to collect the corpses that lined the roadsides. Throughout Rwanda, mass rape and looting accompanied the slaughter. Drunken militia bands, fortified with assorted drugs from ransacked pharmacies, were bused from massacre to massacre. Radio announcers reminded listeners not to take pity on women and children."[2]

Much of the rest of the world was ready to dismiss the Rwanda killing as "tribal" conflict. Fergal Keane, who covered Rwanda for the BBC, wrote: "The fact that this was an act of systematically planned mass murder, a final solution of monstrous proportions, was too often lost in the rush to blame the catastrophe on the old bogey of tribalism. This was not just lazy journalism, it was an insult to the nearly one million dead."[3] Philip Gourevitch noted that "when one read the papers, it didn't seem to me to make much sense. It was described as anarchy and chaos, which struck me as implausible simply because in order to kill at that clip requires organization, it requires method, it requires mobilization. It requires the opposite of anarchy and chaos. Mass destruction is not arbitrary, it doesn't come about willy-nilly."[4]

To label the genocide in Rwanda as "tribalism" is inaccurate, with overtones of racism. News coverage can easily slip into reliance on such stereotyping. A public that is not particularly knowledgeable about the world may accept such images without much questioning. Guarding against that is an important task for today's global journalists. This requires that increased sophistication be built into all aspects of international news gathering–planning the coverage, reporting, and editing. News stories should reflect the complex reality of their subjects. To provide anything less reinforces simplistic notions that undermine the intellectual integrity of the news.

Two months after the killing began, the U.S. government was still looking for principles. On June 10, State Department spokeswoman Christine Shelly said, "Based on the evidence we have seen from observations on the ground, we have every reason to believe that acts of genocide have occurred in Rwanda." But, she added, "clearly not all of the killings that have taken place in Rwanda are killings to which you might apply that label." A reporter asked, "How many 'acts of genocide' does it take to make genocide?" Shelly responded: "That's just not a question that I'm in a position to answer."[5]

The reason for the semantic sleight of hand could be found in the United Nations Convention on the Prevention and Punishment of the Crime of Genocide, which had been approved by the United Nations in 1948 (although not signed by the United States until forty years later). The killing in Rwanda clearly fell within the Convention's definition of genocide: "acts committed with intent to destroy, in whole or in part, a national, ethnical, racial, or religious group." The Convention also states that "the Contracting Parties," which by 1994 included the United States, "confirm that genocide, whether committed in time of peace or in time of war, is a crime under international law which they undertake to prevent and to punish." In other words, the United States–as well as many other nations–was committed by this agreement to respond to genocide. But "acts of genocide" . . . well, maybe that was another matter.

The Clinton administration could afford this waffling because there was little evidence of the public's desire to do anything more. A *Time*/CNN poll in May had found that only 34 percent of respondents favored doing something to stop the violence, while 51 percent opposed any action.[6]

News organizations minimized the use of "genocide" in their reports. Headlines referred to "massacre," "civil war," "fierce clashes," and the like. Alain Destexhe of Doctors Without Borders wrote that "it took three weeks from 6 April–a long time in the world of CNN-style news–before editorials finally began comparing the situation in Rwanda with Germany under Nazism and referring to it as genocide."[7]

The UN Security Council also avoided the word "genocide" in its 1994 resolution condemning "all the breaches of international humanitarian law in Rwanda" including "the killing of members of an ethnic group." Like the American policymakers, UN officials felt no pressure from the public to take a stronger stand. Journalist Linda Melvern observed that "with a consequent lack of moral outcry about genocide it was made easier for politicians to claim that the hatred in Rwanda was impervious to military intervention, and that public opinion was not prepared to pay the price of casualties."[8]

In mid-May, the United Nations finally agreed to send 5,500 troops to Rwanda after the Security Council passed a resolution stating that "acts of genocide may have been committed." But deployment stalled because of disagreements about logistics and finances. Meanwhile, the International Red Cross estimated that 500,000 Rwandans had already been killed.

By this time in Rwanda, a Tutsi army–the Rwanda Patriotic Front–had swept into its homeland from Uganda, captured Kigali, and pushed large numbers of Hutus into Zaire and Tanzania. In refugee centers, such as the huge Goma camp, cholera and other diseases took hold, adding another dimension to the region's misery. Alain Destexhe wrote, "Goma was a hell on earth with cholera killing thousands of people every day." He reported that during the first two weeks, 50,000 people died–5 percent of the camp's refugee population.[9]

Throughout these deadly months, news coverage ranged from the superficial and erratic to the substantive and passionate. Humanitarian aid official Andrew Natsios wrote that the reporting "was extensive, more accidentally than by design, as reporters were returning from coverage of President Nelson Mandela's inauguration [in South Africa] just as the atrocities accelerated and were diverted by their editors to report on the crisis."[10]

Much of the coverage assumed traditional patterns. The extrication of the small number of Europeans trapped in Rwanda received lots of attention, as did the arithmetic of death: body counts serve journalism's desire to quantify. Political issues and other factors behind the killing were treated less thoroughly because they did not lend themselves to the simplistic formulations on which many in the news media rely.

What emerged was a picture of violence in the foreground, with race casting an ominous shadow over the events depicted. Fergal Keane wrote: "In our world of instant televised horror it can become easy to see a black body in almost abstract terms, as part of the huge smudge of eternally miserable blackness that has loomed in and out of the public mind through the decades: Biafra in the sixties; Uganda in the seventies; Ethiopia in the eighties; and now Rwanda in the nineties. We are fed a diet of starving children, of stacked corpses and battalions of refugees, and in the end we find ourselves despising the continent of Africa because it shames us."[11]

Shame is the undercurrent running through many of the appraisals of the world's response to Rwanda. UNAMIR commander Romeo Dallaire wrote: "I made sure that the media were fully supported in all aspects, even at the risk of my personnel, in order to ensure that they could get their gruesome stories out every day. We had to try to shame the international community into action."[12]

For those journalists who extensively covered the killing in Rwanda, the pressure of the horrors they saw was enormous. Fergal Keane wrote: "To witness genocide is to feel not only the chill of your own mortality, but the degradation of all humanity. I am not worried if this sounds like a sermon. I do not care if there are those who dismiss it as emotional or simplistic. It is the fruit of witness. Our trade may be full of imperfections and ambiguities, but if we ignore evil we become the authors of a guilty silence."[13] ABC's Jim Wooten wrote that being in the midst of ubiquitous death was "an excruciating dilemma: at last a reality so wretched it demanded some degree of personal involvement; and yet a story whose wretchedness was of such epic proportions that any personal involvement was useless."[14]

Wooten's comments were made after reporting from the refugee camps in Zaire. This part of the story drew heavy coverage due to a number of factors: the wrenching images of disease and death that television executives know will get an audience's attention; the role of the United States and other nations that were willing to provide humanitarian aid even though they had refused or obstructed military assistance earlier; the apparently straightforward story of suffering refugees.

But the story was really not so straightforward. Many of the refugees were not fleeing Rwanda as victims, but as perpetrators. They had participated in the killing and now, fearing the vengeance of the Tutsi army, the RPF, they reestablished themselves outside their country. Granted, there were many innocents among the hundreds of thousands, and many of these fell to disease, but as Donatella Lorch of the *New York Times* pointed out, "it was the responsibility of the editors and their reporters to constantly remind the public of the connection between the genocide and the epidemic."[15] Philip Gourevitch wrote that the Hutus used refugee camps to regroup and continue their war against the Tutsis: "They began to kill people systematically across Eastern Zaire and they were raiding into Rwanda. . . . These refugee organizations were blindly going on, building up, fattening up, this army of genocide."[16] Fergal Keane wrote: "The story of the refugee camps dominated the world news for much of May, June, and July. The plight of the displaced Hutus became the focus of attention and the genocide a side issue."[17]

Few if any journalists were purposely trying to downplay the Rwandan genocide. But they arrived late; many of them had not been in Rwanda to see the machete-hacked bodies there. When they saw the terrible conditions in the camps, saw children and others dying before their eyes, few of them had already endured the nightmares that came with covering Rwanda itself. And so they let this current tragedy push aside some of the reality of the larger tragedy that had preceded it.

This failure to provide reportorial context is a product of compassion without knowledge. The starkness of events does not mean that they lack complexity, and the ability to tell a story using graphic images does not ensure the emergence of truth. The horrors of the refugee camps in Goma and elsewhere were very real, but they were only part of the story. Good journalism tells more—as much of the story as possible.

This kind of coverage affects political institutions, NGOs, and others, sometimes usefully, sometimes not. One report addressing the international response to Rwanda returned a mixed verdict on the news coverage: "Inadequate and inaccurate reporting by the international media on the genocide itself contributed to international indifference and inaction. Intense media coverage of certain aspects of emergency relief operations, particularly in Goma, influenced both political decision makers and agencies to make ad hoc decisions that were not always in line with sound operating principles and resulted in a skewed emphasis on some relief activities at the expense of others. . . . However, international media coverage also influenced agencies to act urgently and responsibly, and raised awareness of politicians and the public at large, which in turn helped to generate funds."[18]

Regardless of the news media's performance, the governments that stood by and watched the genocide deserved the most criticism. The Organization of African Unity issued a report in 2000 stating that "a small number of major actors could directly have prevented, halted, or reduced the slaughter. They include France in Rwanda itself; the United States at the Security Council; Belgium, whose soldiers knew they could save countless lives if they were allowed to remain in the country; and Rwanda's church leaders."[19] UNAMIR commander General Romeo Dallaire said that 5,000 peacekeepers could have saved 500,000 lives. He wrote that rules of engagement for peacekeepers had been needed that "would permit the force to take offensive action, including the use of deadly force, to prevent genocidal killing. In concert with the application of force where necessary, all the rear-area noncombatants would be disarmed and their weapons collected and controlled by the intervening force."[20]

Some of the political leaders who could have acted but didn't later admitted their mistakes. In March 1998, UN secretary general Kofi Annan said: "The failure to prevent the 1994 genocide was local, national, international, including [UN] member states with capacity. It was our collective failure. . . . We all failed Rwanda."[21] Bill Clinton went to Rwanda in 1998 and accepted a share of the responsibility for inaction: "We did not act quickly enough after the killings began. We should not have allowed the refugee camps to become safe havens for the killers. We did not immediately call these crimes by their rightful name: genocide. . . . It may seem strange to you here, especially the many of you who lost members of your family, but all over the world there were people like me sitting in offices, day after day after day, who did not fully appreciate the depth and the speed with which you were being engulfed by this unimaginable terror."[22]

Clinton did not explain *why* he did not appreciate what was happening. It certainly could not have been because he was inadequately informed. Even if the public was unaware, or at least uninterested, about events in central Africa, there was certainly enough news coverage, diplomatic and intelligence information, and input from NGOs such as the International Committee of the Red Cross to alert policymakers. Kofi

Annan spoke to this in 1998: "The fundamental failure was lack of political will, not the lack of information. If it is lack of information that prevents action, that prevents the solution of crises, then I think we would have very few crises in the world today."[23]

The killing in Rwanda was notable for its volume and speed, but it was not an isolated case. News media performance in other murderous African crises has remained inconsistent. Philip Gourevitch noted that during the first nine months of 1996, "the fact that the Mobutist-Hutu Power alliance in eastern Zaire was slaughtering thousands of people and forcing hundreds of thousands more from their homes did not seem to excite the international press." He noted that the *New York Times* ran only one dispatch about the situation and the *Washington Post*'s coverage was limited to two freelance opinion pieces.[24]

Even when there is coverage, the public might not respond. Addressing the situation in Burundi in 1996, UN spokesperson Sylvana Foa said, "Unfortunately, it is not until we see babies being macheted to death on TV that public opinion forces their governments into action."[25] But even that may overstate the response, particularly in terms of substantive policymaking. As Susan Moeller noted in *Compassion Fatigue:* "Humanitarianism is a smokescreen behind which the United States can hide its political and military neglect. Tragedies shown in print and on television spur relief convoys much more readily than they markedly change foreign policy."[26]

For their part, members of the news audience—the supposed source of pressure on governments—also react inconsistently. Elizabeth Kastor wrote in the *Washington Post* that "each day we turn on the TV, open the paper and decide which new shards of information we will admit into our lives, what cruelties we will contemplate, for whom we will feel empathy. . . . And so we become inured to it, or attempt somehow to respond, all the while striking bargains with ourselves about how much we will let in."[27]

Even with all the after-the-fact examination of events in Rwanda and of the international community's inadequate response, attitudes among the politically powerful have changed little. During the second 2000 presidential debate between George W. Bush and Al Gore, the candidates were asked about Rwanda, "Was it a mistake not to intervene?" Bush said: "I think the administration did the right thing in that case, I do. It was a horrible situation. No one liked to see it on our TV screens. . . . I thought [the administration] made the right decision not to send

U.S. troops into Rwanda." Gore answered: "I think in retrospect we were too late getting in there. We would have saved more lives if we had acted earlier. But I do not think that it was an example of a conflict where we should have put our troops in to try to separate the parties."[28]

Both candidates' responses were notable for their shallowness. Neither man suggested ways in which the United States might have helped, such as by facilitating meaningful UN intervention. The issue in such cases is not simply whether to commit American forces, but rather concerns broader leadership. Former Agency for International Development official Andrew Natsios wrote, "The U.S. national interest in the post–Cold War world requires more precise definition, one that considers the consequences to the country's influence and image in the world if it remains passive in the chaos generated by complex humanitarian emergencies."[29]

Regardless of the impact news coverage may have on policy, journalists could help enlighten those who think that death in Africa may be dismissed as merely a freakish aspect of the natural order of things. But the tone, substance, and volume of coverage must change if that is to happen.

Subsurface racism contributes to the view that war such as that in Rwanda is inevitable tribal bloodletting. Some news organizations reinforce this idea by presenting conflict in Africa as fascinating horror to be viewed safely from afar. The implicit message at the root of that attitude is "These are savages, not worth much of our attention, and certainly not our intervention." Even with the gloss of heroic reporting and graphic pictures, that message can get through to the news audience and officials, affecting public opinion and giving policymakers cover for their inaction.

No matter how cleverly governments may disavow responsibility, and no matter how unconcerned the public may be, journalists must still tell stories such as that of Rwanda. If those stories have little effect, tell more.

The current state of the news business works against this. With a prejudice against stories from abroad—especially from little-known places of negligible strategic importance—getting news organizations to cover these stories is increasingly difficult, at least until the situation has become so horrible that it can no longer be ignored. The role of the news media as a sophisticated early warning system, alerting the public and policymakers to crises before they become tragedies, has become virtually obsolete. The preference now is for "parachute journalism," which involves sending often inadequately informed reporters into situations already at full boil. They may work hard and deliver dramatic stories, but that is not the best possible news product. It tends to lack context and gives its audience a sense that the issues involved are less complex than they really are.

Another obstacle for journalists is the tendency for news executives to rely heavily on cues from government: if the policymakers explicitly or implicitly define a particular situation as unimportant, then news organizations are likely to decide that it doesn't merit much coverage. That approach, however, is a clear abdication of journalistic responsibility. The government's agenda should not be the news media's agenda, particularly when there exists any evidence that officials are neglecting important matters for reasons of political convenience.

Would faster and more thorough coverage of Rwanda by more news organizations have saved lives? That is impossible to answer with certainty, but it might have. Even a slim possibility that news reports might mitigate such a tragedy is reason enough for the news business to reexamine its commitment to coverage of this kind of story.

Beyond Rwanda

As years have passed, the war in Rwanda has become a symbol of the costs of inaction. The Clinton apology underscored the belated recognition by at least one of the world's major powers that horrible events had taken place while it stood by.

If the Rwanda tragedy had been an isolated occurrence, perhaps even the long-overdue acknowledgement of nonfeasance could be viewed as a constructive step toward preventing such disasters in the future. The Rwanda genocide was not, however, an aberration. In Africa and elsewhere, millions of people were and are being killed and millions more uprooted. The U.S. Committee for Refugees reported that in 1999 nearly 7 million people in twenty-four countries fled their homes to escape wars, other violence, and persecution. The list of the countries of refugees fleeing violence in that one year spans the globe:

- Kosovo: 1,000,000
- Congo-Brazzaville: 800,000
- East Timor: 750,000
- Chechnya: 500,000

- Angola: 500,000
- Congo-Kinshasa: 400,000
- Burundi: 400,000
- Afghanistan: 350,000
- Ethiopia: 350,000
- Eritrea: 350,000

These new victims were part of the world's 35 million refugees in 1999: 14 million outside their home countries, and 21 million displaced within their own nations.[30]

The magnitude of this uprooting receives little acknowledgment from most governments or the public. Perhaps the numbers are beyond comprehension, or maybe the problem is so huge that it seems insoluble. Governments sometimes stir themselves to act, often quietly and not always in the most coherent or effective ways. Blaine Harden of the *New York Times* wrote: "What anti-communism was to the Cold War, conscience is to a world of endless small wars. The 38 UN peacekeeping missions launched since 1988 amounts to more than twice the number in the preceding 40 years."[31] That may sound encouraging, but peacekeeping missions vary greatly in their adequacy. There was a peacekeeping mission in Rwanda during the early days of slaughter, so lacking in strength and mandate and so dismally ineffective that it might as well have not been there at all.

Especially in Africa, wars rage and their victims suffer without attracting the world's attention, much less intervention. In Sudan, 1.5 million people—one out of every five southern Sudanese—have died in a war in which, wrote journalist Scott Peterson, "there has never been a defining moment" that might capture the world's interest. "No threat of famine has been so dire," Peterson reported, "no battle so decisive, no mass killing so graphically recorded that it ever caused lasting outrage—or action, or even more than passing interest—in foreign capitals."[32]

A slow-moving, low-tech war in a place few people know about, fought for reasons few outsiders understand, lacks the quality that journalism—especially television journalism—values most: graphic drama. With little chance of holding an audience, coverage of such conflicts is unlikely. Given the costs required to gather and present that information, and given the intense competitive pressures in the news business, telling Sudan's story is too economically risky. The notion that the news audience *should* be told is not determinative. Even the prospect that coverage could affect policy or at least stimulate private assistance to relief organizations does not offset the news industry's leanings toward stories that fit conventional audience-friendly formats. Global journalism remains very selective in what it provides the public.

Sierra Leone

Sierra Leone has been the site of another under-covered African conflict. Because of this vicious civil war, wrote Jim Hoagland in the *Washington Post,* "Sierra Leone has become the world's heart of horror, put on the news map by [rebel leader Foday] Sankoh's use of amputations, gang rape, and forcing children to massacre their own families."[33] Because virtually no country outside Africa had any vital interest threatened by the fighting, there was little inclination to act, no matter how horrible the situation was for thousands of innocents.

As a matter of policy, the most expeditious way for the major powers to respond with some effect was to rely on intervention by a force composed of troops from several African nations. With financial and perhaps logistical support from major powers, this approach might prove useful when the big countries don't want to get their own hands dirty. Blaine Harden wrote in the *New York Times* that "in countries like Sierra Leone, where peacekeeping demands a willingness to wage war, Democratic Man has three stark choices if he wants to salve his conscience: Fight, pay someone else to fight, or stay home and wait for an easier peace to come."[34] The first option is usually politically unappealing, the third allows suffering to proceed indefinitely, leaving the second as the most pragmatic choice.

Relying on mercenaries may seem an unprincipled way to avoid committing a nation's own troops, but paying for foreign soldiers to be put at risk is *politically* less expensive than sending one's own into danger. The practice is nothing new, and it may be a reasonable policy if handled carefully—meaning that the intervention force is trained and commanded well enough so that it will alleviate rather than exacerbate the problems it has been sent to address. Kofi Annan has said that he has been tempted to use "private security firms" as a UN rapid reaction force. But, he decided, "the world may not be ready to privatize peace."[35]

The Clinton administration created the Africa Crisis Response Initiative to help African militaries be prepared to respond to conflict in the region. The U.S. commitment was small: as of the end of 2000, just $20 million a year was allotted, 6,500 troops were trained, and only nonlethal equipment, such as communications gear, was provided.[36] This is a minimalist approach that probably will do more to salve American conscience than to promote African peace. To reduce the chances of conflict, the stability of African nations must be reinforced through a realistic long-term commitment of meaningful military assistance and, more important, substantive economic aid and debt relief.

There is something intrinsically condescending about the Western powers using NATO forces in the Balkans while refusing to participate in significant peacekeeping operations in Africa. One way to look at it is, predominantly white nations will send their soldiers to protect white people, while black Africans must wait for black African troops. Blaine Harden wrote that "in Africa, the bar for intervention that risks casualties has been set very much higher. Part of the reason is the region's negligible economic and strategic significance."[37] Along these lines, Jim Hoagland wrote: "Economically, the developed world has long abandoned Africa to a fate outside the new global era. In a world of fiber optics and computers, the continent's copper, base metals, and other commodities no longer justify the kind of deep involvement that Britain, France, and the United States once practiced."[38]

These economic and security concerns are logical determinants of policy, but they are cold-blooded. They are abstractions when compared to the human suffering that is not addressed. Journalists such as Jim Hoagland and Blaine Harden in the case of Sierra Leone raise issues that the public should consider, regardless of policymakers' priorities.

News organizations should also consider the criteria on which decisions about comprehensiveness of coverage are based. Not all readers see the newspaper every day; not every listener or viewer hears or watches newscasts daily; and Web surfers miss stories. Without a commitment by news organizations to cover important events thoroughly and consistently enough to make likely their being seen by a significantly large audience, the public will not be properly informed.

Some coverage may be better than no coverage, and there are limits to news organizations' resources. But without even getting into the question of whether there is an implicit professional mandate for "humanitarian journalism," there certainly is a baseline level of information that is needed for news consumers to be able to make judgments about events throughout the world. In the coverage of most of the recent conflicts in Africa, even these basic standards have not been met by most news organizations.

This is a particularly acute issue in the United States, given the significance of race in past and present American society. Jesse Jackson wrote: "Sierra Leone provided the ancient homelands for many slaves who were brought primarily to South Carolina, North Carolina, and parts of Georgia. We have as many if not more cultural and ethnic ties to Western Africa as we do to the Balkans." Concerning the disparities in American responses to Africa and Yugoslavia, Jackson wrote: "There is a massive and telling difference in how we have responded politically and how the media have covered the two crises. In Yugoslavia and bordering countries, a virtual city of reporters has provided coverage. In Sierra Leone, CNN didn't even send a camera to cover the signing of the historic cease-fire."[39] On another occasion, Jackson said, "If Americans had seen Sierra Leoneans walking down the street amputated, babies bludgeoned, and pregnant women stabbed, Americans would have been as upset over Sierra Leone as they were over Kosovo."[40]

Even when the pictures Jackson described did appear in news reports, they usually did so without context. A montage of horror can shock profoundly, but its effects are unlikely to linger or produce constructive response if those who see it are not provided with adequate explanation of why the events happened and what might be done about them. Again, a comparison of Sierra Leone and the Balkans is instructive. After a trip to Sierra Leone, *Washington Post* managing editor Steve Coll wrote: "In Kosovo, the middle-class status and racial features of the victims, as well as echoes of Europe's Holocaust, allowed many Americans to empathize with the Kosovars, to feel and imagine what happens when armies loose themselves on civilians. . . . But in Sierra Leone, outside engagement with the war came to be dominated by pity-inducing, context-empty images of the limbless, whether in media coverage or during visits by politicians to Freetown's rehabilitation camps for amputees. These stripped-down, politics-free pictures of armless victims helped to consign Sierra Leone's war to the mental box many Americans reserve for Africa. Few understood, for example, that most of Freetown's victims were as urban and middle class as Pristina's."[41]

The mental box and lack of understanding that Coll cited are partly attributable to racial attitudes that are grounded in stereotypes. News coverage can clear away some of this intellectual debris, but only if the coverage is not based on the same assumptions and does not fall into the same traps that may ensnare an underinformed public.

East Timor

Policymakers must similarly resist the allure of ill-considered conventional wisdom. The current reluctance to participate in armed intervention is based partly on the idea that intervention simply doesn't work. Poorly planned intervention that is preceded by bluff and bluster probably *won't* work. But there is evidence that resolute action can, in certain circumstances, be helpful, even if belated. East Timor is a case in point.

The island of Timor, comprising roughly 13,000 square miles, is 1,300 miles east of Jakarta and about 400 miles northwest of Darwin, Australia. In 1949, the Dutch transferred the western half of the island to Indonesia, and in 1975 Portugal withdrew from the eastern half. After the Portuguese left, Indonesia took control and suppressed an independence movement. Between 1975 and the late 1980s, about 200,000 East Timorese died from violence, hunger, and disease.

The independence movement struggled on, and in 1996 two of its advocates, Bishop Carlos Ximenes Belo and Jose Ramos-Horta, won the Nobel Peace Prize. After the fall of Indonesia's President Suharto, the new president, Bacharuddin Jusuf Habibie, was preoccupied with economic and political problems and in January 1999 he agreed to allow the Timorese to hold a referendum about autonomy. During the months leading up to the referendum, militias linked to the Indonesian military terrorized East Timor, but when the voting took place in August 1999, a 98 percent turnout voted 80 percent in favor of breaking away from Indonesia. That spurred the militias to new levels of violence, killing, looting, and burning their way across East Timor and driving several hundred thousand residents into the hills or into West Timor.[42]

The world saw little of this because almost all the journalists who had been in East Timor left when UN personnel pulled out as the violence was accelerating. Some journalists were caught up in the chaos. BBC reporter Jonathan Head was beaten by militia members, and another BBC correspondent, Matt Frei, reported seeing a living person being chopped to pieces: "It took only 30 seconds. . . . The attack was so ferocious that bits of him were literally flying off. The sound reminded me of a butcher's shop, the thud of cleaved meat. I'll never forget it."[43] After most news organizations had pulled their people out, a handful of journalists remained, including photographer Max Stahl, whose video of women and children fleeing the militias provided the only pictures to emerge from this phase of the East Timor crisis.[44]

Although the referendum results and the post-election violence were predictable, the United Nations was not prepared to respond. The United Nations had encouraged the independence effort generally and the referendum in particular, but failed to protect the East Timorese against the militias and their Indonesian allies.

Within days of the voting, the Rwanda-type pattern of inaction changed. East Timor's neighbor, Australia, and its former colonial proprietor, Portugal, demanded that the Security Council act. Australia offered to lead a peacekeeping force. On September 15–just two weeks after the East Timor referendum–the Security Council authorized intervention by "a coalition of the willing," and five days later the first troops went ashore.[45]

A strong case can be made that the United Nations should have mounted a forceful presence in East Timor during the run-up to the voting and thereby perhaps have deterred the violence. But when compared with the sluggish reaction to other crises, the relative promptness and effectiveness of the intervention provided evidence that "peacekeeping" (or, more accurately, imposing a relative degree of peace) is feasible. If individual nations with the will and the muscle to act show some resolve, bureaucratic inertia might be broken. (After the fact, some would challenge Australia's motives in East Timor, pointing to Australia's claim, based on a 1989 deal with Indonesia, to half of East Timor's oil and gas reserves. Although Australia reported spending $500 million on peacekeeping and $40 million on humanitarian aid in East Timor, the United Nations would not accept the claim to the oil and gas. In late 2000, Australia and East Timor were devising a compromise.[46])

The Witness Speaks

News coverage may be a factor in building the resolve to intervene. In humanitarian crises, *how* the news media cover events can be crucial. A spokesman for the International Committee of the Red Cross said: "Probably never before has the fine art of communication had so much power of life and death over so many people. . . . We [in the ICRC] are increasingly aware of the phenomenal weight a word, a sentence, an expressed belief can have."[47]

Words may be powerful, but only if used correctly. When the issue involves confronting the realities of genocide, collective denial–by the news media among others–is not uncommon. University of Virginia professor Michael J. Smith wrote: "In this world of denial, genocide is not genocide, but 'civil conflict'; murderous removal of people not genocidal ethnic cleansing but 'population resettlement'; and merciless bombing of civilians not terrorism but 'civil war.' Responsibility to gather accurate information and to face the worst of its grim implications must be shared among all the players in the global arena, and we must all be vigilant about the possibility of manipulating both images and negotiations for purposes of hiding, or continuing to perpetrate, awful horrors. To these pitfalls of manipulation, we must add our own constant temptation willfully to avert our gaze from events that shock our collective conscience."[48]

Although it may be natural for those who see the worst of human behavior to hope that they are wrong, that what they have seen is not really as bad as it appears, such wishful thinking can be counterproductive. Depending on the stakes involved, such caution may not be a good thing in journalism. Just as mistakenly alarmist reporting can be harmful, so too can unduly restrained appraisals mislead those who are relying on journalists' judgment.

Ideally, timely and assertive news coverage serves justice. But questions remain about the scope of journalists' duties. Does the journalist have a responsibility to step beyond traditional news venues and provide information elsewhere, such as in a courtroom? News professionals are extremely cautious about this, even when reporters are asked to help in the prosecution of alleged war criminals. Paul Tash, executive editor of the *St. Petersburg Times* and chair of the American Society of Newspaper Editors Freedom of Information Committee, has said that journalists "should try to keep themselves as observers in the process rather than participants in it. . . . I would say that in an extremely rare and compelling case, a reporter's or photographer's obligation as a citizen may outweigh the desire to preserve our independence from the judicial process."[49]

That cautious approach has been endorsed by Richard Goldstone, first prosecutor at the International Criminal Tribunals for the Former Yugoslavia and Rwanda: "As international tribunals are established, journalism has gained a new and as yet undefined dimension. Journalists have very different mandates, modes of operating, routes to access information, and thresholds of proof in comparison with judicial bodies. The two functions should not be confused. It is important that reporters stay reporters—that is, uncover and write the story (and the story behind the story) for the general public. . . . Like aid workers and Red Cross or

Red Crescent delegates, if reporters become identified as would-be witnesses, their safety and future ability to be present at a field of battle will be compromised. . . . They should not be compelled to testify lest they should give up their ability to work in the field, but they may of course testify voluntarily."[50]

On occasion, journalists have decided to do just that. In August 1992, Ed Vulliamy of *The Guardian* and an ITN (Independent Television News) crew were the first journalists to enter the Serb-run Omarska concentration camp in Bosnia. In 1996, he was asked to testify before the International Criminal Tribunal for the Former Yugoslavia at The Hague about crimes allegedly committed at Omarska and elsewhere by Serb combatant Dusko Tadic. Vulliamy later wrote: "I decided this was a chance for some kind of reckoning for the only people I really cared about–the victims. I threw aside any pretense of neutrality and went to The Hague. I gave the prosecution in the Tadic case all my notebooks and I told them everything I knew."[51]

He explained his decision by arguing for the importance of a moral imperative in the journalist's work, echoing sentiments expressed by other reporters who had felt excessively constrained by "objectivity" in the face of great evil. Vulliamy wrote, "I believe that there are moments in history when neutrality is not neutral, but complicit in the crime." In Bosnia, Rwanda, and elsewhere, he continued, "the neutrality adopted by diplomats and the media is both dangerous and morally reprehensible. By remaining neutral, we reward the bullies of history and discard the peace and justice promised us by the generation that defeated the Third Reich. We create a mere intermission before the next round of atrocities. There are times when we as reporters have to cross the line, recognize right as right, wrong as wrong, and stand up to be counted."[52]

If disengagement is considered indispensable to objectivity, then Vulliamy is clearly breaking away from a traditional journalistic standard. But an argument can be made that certain moral responsibilities–such as testifying in a war crimes trial–are more important than rigid adherence to such standards. There is no precise formula to determine where the line is drawn, and, as Richard Goldstone observed, journalists should safeguard their information-gathering prerogatives. The balancing act is difficult.

The problems that might arise were underscored when Vulliamy testified in another International Criminal Tribunal trial. In this one, the defendant was Milan Kovacevic, who had set up and managed several Serb concentration camps. On the stand, Vulliamy was instructed by the judges to read aloud some interview notes. "That seemed perfectly reasonable," he wrote, "but then the lawyers demanded to see all my notebooks and insisted on seeing pages adjacent to the Kovacevic interview to establish 'context.' They dove at an address and telephone number written in the margin, demanding to know whose details I had jotted down. My colleagues' warnings echoed in my ear. The phone number was extremely sensitive; indeed its owner in clear danger from these vultures."[53]

By testifying, Vulliamy had gone beyond standard journalistic practice and, as a result, a source was jeopardized. If one reporter burns a source, even inadvertently, other journalists' news gathering may be impaired. That is a substantial price, but some journalists may judge it to be reasonable given the substance of a war crimes trial. Vulliamy went on to testify in other trials at The Hague. By mid-2001, he had delivered more prosecution testimony than any other witness.[54]

While Vulliamy and some other journalists testified before the International Tribunal, the news media collectively showed little interest in the proceedings. Christian Chartier, a spokesperson for the tribunal, said, "We tried to make provisions for television coverage." But, he added, the trials "did not provide the spectacle the media wanted. The big problem we have is that the trials take a very long time."[55] The importance of the subject matter was not enough to overcome journalism's instinctive recoiling in the face of complexity. The world could have used some reminding a few years after the discovery of Omarska, Trnopolje, and other concentration camps, and those convicted of war crimes deserved to have their evil exposed to public scrutiny, but for many news organizations these are not priorities.

More thorough coverage might also dissolve some people's biases about the trials. If a Bosnian Croat, for instance, is convicted of a war crime, other Bosnian Croats may think he was railroaded, particularly if they have received little honest news coverage of the proceedings. BBC radio producer Henri Astier wrote that "the dearth of information coming out of The Hague does nothing to promote the tribunal's aim of reconciliation or to reassure people that its decisions are based solely on the facts and the law."[56]

Astier also made a good point about the existing coverage of war crimes trials. He noted that "the media, which in domestic cases usually acts as a powerful check on the accusatorial powers of the state, play the opposite role in cases of war crimes. Some of the bias is unthinking.

Phrases like 'indicted war criminal' are used routinely."[57] The presumption of innocence should not be discarded by reporters, regardless of the magnitude of the alleged offense. As a matter of law—and as a matter of good journalism—one may be charged with war crimes, but no one is a "war criminal" until a court delivers that verdict.

Coverage of the international tribunals would make more complete the reporting that began during the atrocities that led to the trials. This is part of the overall story and should not be neglected. Also, the tribunals' proceedings have illustrated how standards of justice are changing. During the trials concerning Rwanda and the former Yugoslavia, rape was formally designated as a crime against humanity and was considered an element of genocide. This overdue step was taken partly as a result of pressure from women judges and investigators. Also, the presence of more women journalists, especially in Bosnia, may have increased the awareness of rape being used as a terrorizing weapon.

In September 1998, Jean-Paul Akayesu, who had been mayor of Taba, Rwanda, was the first person to be convicted of the crime of genocide under international law. Sentenced to varying terms of imprisonment on numerous counts, Akayesu ended up with a cumulative sentence of life imprisonment. (Testimony from two journalists was cited in the judgment.) Rape was one of the specific offenses of which Akayesu was found guilty. In its judgment, the Tribunal said that "rape is a form of aggression . . . and rape in fact constitutes torture" when inflicted by, or at the instigation of, or with the consent of a public official or a person acting in an official capacity.[58]

In February 2001, the International Criminal Tribunal addressing events in the former Yugoslavia convicted three former Bosnian Serb soldiers of rape and sexual slavery. The verdict was the first to specifically define rape as a crime against humanity, a more serious level of offense than torture. This case involved low-ranking soldiers, but the judgment underscored the magnitude of rape as a tactic. Human rights investigators for the European Union and other organizations estimated that in Bosnia in 1992 alone, 20,000 Muslim women and girls were raped by Serbs.[59]

Also, UN officials reported in early 2001 that they had found patterns of sexual violence as a tool of war in East Timor. One of the problems facing investigators and reporters covering this issue is the lack of clarity of the statistics about these crimes. Relying on numbers can lead to understating the magnitude of what had happened. David

Senior, the UN's chief sex crimes investigator, said: "How do you put a number on five women being raped by twelve guys? How do you put a number on a woman being raped daily for six months? How do you put a number on one girl being raped by three guys for five nights? For me, numbers don't describe the impact that rape has had on the women of East Timor."[60] This illustrates the need for news organizations to resist the desire to quantify when the numbers might mislead.

Perhaps it is a sign of incremental progress that crimes against women are being treated more seriously. As investigations proceed, the systematic and widespread use of rape as an instrument of genocidal terror is being increasingly well documented in Rwanda, Bosnia, and other war zones. Given this pervasiveness and the war crimes tribunals' more assertive response to charges of rape, the news media should follow suit by expanding coverage of this particular form of barbarism when it is encountered.

Another aspect of the Rwanda trials that deserves notice is the guilty verdict in June 2000 in the case of a journalist who showed how "news" can pervert morality. Belgian-born Georges Ruggiu, in news broadcasts on Rwanda's Radio Television Libre des Mille Collines, had "incited [listeners] to kill" Tutsis. After pleading guilty and expressing remorse, Ruggiu was sentenced to twelve years in prison.[61] In its judgment, the Tribunal cited as precedent the case of Julius Streicher, publisher of the anti-Semitic newspaper *Der Stuermer,* who was convicted by the Nuremberg Tribunal of "incitement to murder and extermination" of Jews. Streicher was sentenced to death and executed in 1946.

In October 2000, another Rwanda tribunal trial began in which three more Rwandan journalists were charged with "public incitement to commit genocide" and other crimes.

The tribunals addressing the crimes against humanity committed in Rwanda and the former Yugoslavia may eventually bring legal closure to the wars in those countries, and as an assertion of the rule of law they have considerable value. Their judgments almost certainly will not, however, eliminate further atrocities. Journalists may feel frustrated and helpless when they cover such events, but their resolve to witness horror and provide information may make possible the resurrection of justice.

The wars in Rwanda, Sierra Leone, East Timor, and elsewhere that are described in this chapter seemed archaic in a world that had learned about the menace of nuclear weapons during the Cold War and had seen technologically sophisticated combat in the Persian Gulf War.

In the Balkans, the next level of the ongoing conflict there would see technological refinements of warfare and news coverage. NATO's advanced weaponry allowed war to become more politically manageable, if militarily less effective. News about the war was disseminated not only in traditional ways, but also on the Internet, which is changing every aspect of the news business.

From machetes to Stealth bombers, from Radio Television Libre des Mille Collines to the World Wide Web, savagery and its coverage were taking on a high-tech gloss.

CHAPTER FIVE

Covering "Humanitarian War"

The grim arrogance underlying Yugoslavia's willingness to go to war with NATO over Kosovo was evident when Yugoslav president Slobodan Milosevic told German foreign minister Joschka Fischer in early 1999, "I can stand death—lots of it—but you can't."[1]

That pronouncement set the tone for NATO's first war—a conflict that established new standards for the exercise of power in Europe and tested technological advances in news coverage.

By the time of the Kosovo War, the world knew about the levels that violence could reach in the Balkans. Reporters covering this latest conflict were not hard-pressed, as they had been during the early fighting in Bosnia, to get the news audience's attention. Nevertheless, journalists faced many challenges. The Clinton administration followed the Gulf War pattern of trying to control the flow and substance of coverage. Terms such as "humanitarian war" and "genocide" were used freely by political leaders trying to garner public support. As this chapter illustrates, the news media had good reason to be alert to manipulation.

The most significant innovation in covering this war was the wide use of the Internet. During this first Web war, standards for online news were tested in matters such as the accuracy of sources and reliability of links. News consumers turned to the Web in unprecedented numbers. This new medium proved its value in getting more information to more people.

Milosevic may have been correct about his adversaries' low tolerance for casualties, but he miscalculated the havoc that could be caused by NATO's modern armory. Although the effectiveness of NATO's air war would be questioned in terms of its direct impact on the situation within Kosovo, there was no doubt that it critically affected Serbia's economic and political life.

This war, like most others, was about territory and power. Milosevic wanted to tie Kosovo to what was left of his Yugoslavia. He intended to bring the ethnic Albanian population of Kosovo to heel, wiping out the independence movement that had annoyed him with its political and military tactics. He was particularly determined to crush the Kosovo Liberation Army, which had carried on a persistent guerrilla war in pursuit of independence. If this crackdown caused problems for other nations, so be it. Michael Ignatieff wrote that Milosevic, never one for subtlety, "perfected a new weapon of war: the use of refugee flows to destabilize neighboring countries, to immobilize the logistics of NATO forces by handing them a humanitarian catastrophe."[2]

Milosevic had revoked Kosovo's limited autonomy in 1989, and gradually chipped away at Kosovars' political and personal freedoms. This prompted periodic warnings from the Bush and Clinton administrations, and eventually led to a U.S. diplomatic effort orchestrated by Richard Holbrooke, who had engineered the 1995 Dayton accords that addressed the conflict in Bosnia. Concerted Serb military action began in early 1998. By May 1999, 90 percent of Kosovo's ethnic Albanians had been displaced—600,000 scattered within Kosovo, and 700,000 outside Kosovo's borders. The U.S. State Department reported that the Serbs' ethnic cleansing violated human rights and humanitarian law in many ways: forced expulsions; looting and burning; detentions; summary executions (in at least seventy towns and villages); rape; violations of medical neutrality (destroying medical facilities and killing doctors); and "identity cleansing," which involved destroying identity papers and anything else that documented the ethnic Albanians' ties to Kosovo.[3]

Months of frustrating diplomatic efforts failed to get Milosevic to back off. Every time he appeared to give some ground, he would then push forward on another front. His intransigence presented NATO with an unprecedented choice: should it make war for the first time in its history, or should it let Milosevic do whatever he wanted within the former Yugoslavia?

NATO began its air war in March 1999, concentrating on military targets in Kosovo and Serbia, plus the Serb infrastructure. To protect NATO air crews, most attacks were launched from at least 15,000 feet, which limited their effectiveness in hitting the small military units and the scattered hardware that the Serbs were using in Kosovo. President Clinton's early announcement that no ground troops would be used removed what would have been the most effective threat to the Serbs' campaign. Nevertheless, Serbia could not withstand the battering NATO administered. After slightly less than three months of air attacks, Milosevic agreed to NATO's demands and the war ended. KFOR, a peacekeeping force of 55,000 NATO troops (including approximately 7,000 Americans and 4,000 Russians) moved into Kosovo.

KFOR's arrival did not mean peace. As Kosovar Albanians returned to their homes, some took revenge on Kosovar Serbs. Now it was these Serbs who took flight: according to United Nations refugee officials, approximately 240,000 Kosovars—mostly Serbs and mostly children—fled during the six months after the war officially ended. Addressing the new violence, Bernard Kouchner, the UN administrator of Kosovo, said, "Some Kosovo Serbs were victims of the Kosovo Liberation Army violations of humanitarian law, but there was nothing close to equivalence" with what the ethnic Albanians had earlier endured.[4] (Albanian dominance also meant the use of Kosova, the Albanian spelling, rather than Kosovo, although the latter remains commonly used in most of the world. There is meaning in a single letter.)

Detailed studies are available that examine the military and political issues of the Kosovo War, particularly as they related to the evolution of post–Cold War Europe. (Among the best is *Winning Ugly: NATO's War to Save Kosovo*, by Ivo Daalder and Michael O'Hanlon.) For the news media, this conflict was more than just a continuation of the Balkan wars that journalists had been covering for nearly twenty years. By this time, Slobodan Milosevic had been indicted for war crimes and his brutal tactics were well-known.

Public disbelief about the savagery of war in the Balkans had largely evaporated, reducing somewhat the burden on journalists not only to report but also to convince. British journalist Maggie O'Kane wrote: "The difference for many of us covering the Kosovar war, who also covered the Bosnian war, was that the justification for risking our lives did not have the same moral imperative and urgency as it did in Bosnia. In Bosnia, there were huge moral obligations to reveal to the world the horror of ethnic cleansing. In Kosovo, we already knew what the Serbs were doing and we had thousands of testimonies from the Kosovar refugees to confirm the horror of this wave of ethnic cleansing. We also had learned from the experience of Bosnia, where a whole generation of journalists had literally risked their lives to expose those stories to an indifferent political establishment."[5]

Although the world had become familiar with Milosevic's penchant for ethnic cleansing, there were other issues that emerged in Kosovo. NATO was establishing rules of conduct for the new Europe. William Safire wrote that the Kosovo war proved that the Western powers were willing "to place humanity's resistance to barbarism above national sovereignty. When a nation commits a mass atrocity against a segment of its own people, other nations have just asserted their right to intervene with force."[6]

But *how* the war was fought raised questions for journalists and others, especially concerning NATO's reluctance to send ground troops into Kosovo to stop the depredations of the Serb military and the savage Serb militias. Having seen the atrocities perpetrated in Kosovo, Maggie O'Kane wrote that "at the back of everybody's mind there is a dirty, little nagging thought that said there's something a little bit sick about the strongest military alliance in the world lacking the political leadership to take on these murderous paramilitary thugs, and instead bombing them from a distance and watching helplessly while hell happens on Kosovo's soil."[7]

How, as well as whether, to intervene will be a critical issue as organizations such as NATO and individual countries such as the United States shape policy in the coming years. Related to this is the larger question of NATO's future. What is the mission of this Cold War institution now that the Cold War is over? The news media can be expected to turn their spotlight on such issues while they address the evolving protocols of gathering information.

Dealing with the Players

War coverage comprises certain consistent elements:

- Journalists must wade through a flood of propaganda from various parties, some of it crafted and disseminated with considerable skill.
- Logistical obstacles and safety concerns may limit reporters' first-hand access to some places where the story is developing.

- Governments will try to make their pronouncements about the conflict less susceptible to challenge by the press in their own countries by applying a gloss of patriotism.

Perhaps more than in any other kind of coverage, war reporting tests journalists' resolve to resist constraints imposed by those behind the news. The Kosovo war was no exception. In the *American Journalism Review*, Sherry Ricchiardi wrote that "disgruntled journalists quickly nicknamed this conflict the 'hearsay war,' replete with stories that included the phrase 'it cannot be independently confirmed.'"[8]

Following the pattern established during the Persian Gulf War, NATO and American officials did their best to control coverage, a task that was both more difficult and more important given the political haze that shrouded the rationale for intervention. Michael Ignatieff wrote: "Kosovo made it obvious that wars waged in the name of values invariably turn out to be more controversial than wars waged for interests. Maintaining popular support for humanitarian intervention required unrelenting media management by NATO and the political leadership of the alliance countries."[9]

General Wesley Clark, supreme allied commander, Europe, was in charge of NATO's military operations and acknowledged the need for this management. "We knew at the outset," he wrote, "that feeding the information machine was critical to sustained public support of the campaign. . . . When the television coverage was incomplete, or the commentary inaccurate, we called to offer information or to request clarifications and corrections."[10]

NATO provided a daily briefing that was televised live to the world on CNN and other cable and satellite networks. Despite Clark's concern about correcting news media errors, NATO itself sometimes got the story wrong. NATO told the press corps that two Kosovo Albanian leaders had been assassinated, but they hadn't been. It took NATO five days to get its story straight about American war planes accidentally attacking a convoy of Kosovar refugees. (Finally a U.S. Air Force general told journalists that some of his pilots may have mistakenly killed civilians.)[11]

The Clinton administration devised an aggressive media strategy that might be called "spin and control." Howard Kurtz of the *Washington Post* wrote that when Secretary of State Madeleine Albright and Secretary of Defense William Cohen appeared on network news shows in March 1999, they were "doing more than pressing the administration's line in time of war. They are demonizing the opposition and carefully controlling the flow of information as part of the all-important battle for public opinion. And they are doing so in a relative news vacuum created by the Serbian expulsion of most Western journalists and the lack of television pictures from the Balkans war zone."[12]

This approach was apparent in the Pentagon's dealings with the press. Department of Defense spokesman Kenneth Bacon said, "The leadership is taking a more conservative approach," and noted that Secretary Cohen and Joint Chiefs chairman General Henry Shelton "think we ought to be as stingy as possible in giving out information, which means we have to be restrained with the press."[13] This restraint reached the point at which some news organizations protested. In April 1999, the *New York Times, Washington Post, Wall Street Journal, Los Angeles Times,* Associated Press, CNN, and NBC sent a letter to Secretary Cohen complaining that "though the ongoing military campaign in the Balkans is one of the largest and most important U.S. military operations conducted in recent years, the Department of Defense has supplied far less information to the media and public than during the Persian Gulf War. . . . At a minimum, we believe the department should make public its information on what targets in Yugoslavia have been hit. . . . The media should be told which planes are involved in operations, how many operations they fly, and the degree of their success." Cohen did not respond, but Pentagon spokesman Bacon held a meeting to listen to the news organizations' complaints.[14] Policy did not appreciably change.

On the other side of the war, the Serbs were also trying to control coverage in ways that would influence international opinion. Slobodan Milosevic understood this process, and, wrote Michael Ignatieff, "instead of fighting NATO in the air, he fought NATO on the air waves. By allowing CNN and the BBC to continue broadcasting from inside Serbia, he hoped to destabilize and unsettle Western opinion with nightly stories of civilians carbonized in bombed trains and media workers incinerated by strikes on television stations."[15] Milosevic's approach had some success in raising doubts about NATO's strategy. Maggie O'Kane wrote: "Television told the uncomfortable truth of lives and limbs blown apart by—horror of horrors—us. This was the price of war, as NATO chose to fight it."[16]

As is the case in many conflicts, casualty figures—especially those used by political leaders to justify intervention—are not always reliable. In 1999, NATO said that 10,000 Kosovar Albanians had been killed by

Serbs. A year later, the International Criminal Tribunal stated that the number was 3,000.[17] News organizations have good reason to be skeptical about any statistics, such as those about civilian casualties, that are virtually impossible to verify.

Truth was a rare commodity everywhere in the war zone, during the bombing and later, when KFOR moved in. Tracy Wilkinson of the *Los Angeles Times* noted that "we expected the Serbs to lie. Serbian officials are masters at lying. But what surprised me was the extent to which the Kosovo Albanians' political leadership also lied."[18] When the Kosovar Albanians unleashed their anger on the Kosovar Serbs, the coverage was less vivid than earlier stories had been that reported Serb atrocities. Balancing relative evils is difficult for journalists. Also, sources can be hard to find when the subject matter does not fit into the story line promoted by officials, which in this case was the purported success of KFOR's peacekeeping efforts. Nevertheless, a story premise of "these are the good guys, those are the bad guys" is likely to be misleadingly simplistic when reporting events such as this.

Another Kosovo story that was carefully nurtured by NATO, and particularly American, officials concerned genocide. In striking contrast to its behavior during the war in Rwanda in 1994, when U.S. officials were extraordinarily careful not to say that genocide was taking place, the Clinton administration used allegations of genocide to bolster support for intervening in Kosovo. Neither the United States nor any other NATO country formally charged Serbia with committing genocide or invoked the 1948 United Nations convention against genocide, which would have triggered UN-mandated action against the Serbs "to prevent" the genocide and "to punish" its perpetrators.

But NATO members, in more general and less legalistic terms, used "genocide" as part of their public rationale for the war.[19] State Department spokesman James Rubin, citing a "mixture of confirmed and unconfirmed reports," declared, "Whether or not the formal definition of genocide has been met, there are indicators that genocide is occurring."[20]

Journalists should proceed carefully when "genocide" becomes part of government officials' wartime litany, especially when these policymakers shy away from invoking the UN juridical process. Claiming that genocide is taking place is an effective way to rally support for a policy that supposedly responds to it. Journalists should challenge government officials who may be using "genocide" as a politically convenient semantic subterfuge.

Casual use of the word diminishes the horrific magnitude of genocide and the suffering that its victims endure. The Holocaust perpetrated by the Nazis and the Hutus' mass murder of Tutsis in Rwanda are generally considered to constitute genocide. The expulsion of the Kosovar Albanians may have put Milosevic in the company of Hitler and Stalin, who also ordered forced deportations of ethnic groups. But if genocide is defined according to the terms of the UN convention, which addresses the "physical destruction" of a population group, then the term might not be applicable to the overall situation in Kosovo.

Regardless of policymakers' semantic choices, if journalists use "genocide," they should understand its meaning and explain it to their audience.

War and the Internet

The Persian Gulf War is often cited as the post-Vietnam standard for wartime news coverage. It was the first war to be covered live by broadcast and cable networks. It was also the first war to be covered so constantly, day in and day out, particularly by CNN, which built its audience and strengthened its claim to journalistic legitimacy during the war.

Eight years later, new players and new technology made this Gulf War standard an anachronism. From news organizations' perspective, the Kosovo War was very different from the Gulf War. The refugee flow into Albania and Macedonia was heavily covered, but there was no massive invasion force built up over several months that invited extensive coverage. The NATO combatants were mostly air crews based in Italy and elsewhere in Europe. Briefings were conducted in Belgium. Some video from within Serbia was available, as was air combat footage provided by NATO.

While CNN had been the dominant American cable news provider during the Gulf War, in Kosovo it was challenged by newcomers MSNBC and Fox News. All three saw their ratings rise substantially during the Kosovo fighting. During the week of March 24–30, 1999–when NATO began bombing Yugoslavia–CNN, which retained the largest cable news audience, saw its overall average audience reach 672,000 households, up 113 percent over the previous week. Its prime-time audience rose to 1,084,000 households, up 79 percent. MSNBC's overall audience was up to 225,000 households and in primetime 348,000 households, increases of 92 and 107 percent. Fox News' overall average viewership reached 114,000 households and in prime time 269,000 households, up 52 and 23 percent.[21]

CNN, along with Britain's Sky News, had an attentive audience among those in Serbia who had satellite television. They watched the daily NATO briefings televised by the networks, looking for hints about likely targets of the next wave of bombing.[22]

While television viewership climbed, the new medium of Internet news also attracted a substantial audience. On the first day of the NATO air strikes, CNN's Web site had 31 million page views. (The site had attracted 34 million page views in 1998 on the day the Starr Report about the Clinton-Lewinsky scandal was released.) For the week, CNN had more than 154 million page views. ABCNEWS.com reported that its number of visitors increased more than 60 percent when the Kosovo combat began. Other news organizations' Web sites also saw large increases in numbers of visitors. These were not just American news consumers. CNN found that Yugoslavs' visits to CNN.com rose 963 percent.[23]

This latter figure underscores the importance of the advent of Web news. It is easily accessible and difficult to block; it cannot be jammed as broadcast signals can be (although access to the Web can, in some instances, be obstructed or monitored). When traditional information channels are suspect because of government restrictions or other reasons, anyone with true Internet access may choose to get news elsewhere.

But even access to the Web does not ensure access to the truth. A new kind of chess game now is played between those who disseminate news and those who want to control it. When the NATO bombing began, the Milosevic government shut down Radio B92, a Belgrade station that was persistently critical of the regime. Veran Matic and Drazen Pantic, who were among the founders of B92, wrote that one week later "the government took over our Web address; anyone going to the B92 Web site would see government propaganda supporting Milosevic's stance against NATO. . . . This is why Radio B92 operates under the slogan 'Don't believe anyone, not even us.'"[24]

The potency of the Web may require a change in military targeting if one side wants to shut down the other's Internet communication. British scholar Philip Taylor wrote that this means that "power, telephonic, and electrical supplies, as well as television stations, have become strategic targets for bombing, much as factories were in World War II." But even that bombing, writes Taylor, cannot defeat the correspondent armed with a computer. "A mobile phone," he notes, "attached to a laptop computer with a modem will bypass this—for as long as the batteries last—suggesting that prolonging battery life might be the most significant twenty-first century development for information warfare."[25]

For news consumers, the Web's first war featured a remarkably diverse array of information sources. There were the sites of major news organizations, such as television networks, newspapers, and magazines. These offered not only the material that appeared on their parents' air or pages, but also the kind of background information that often gets squeezed out of the daily news package (a particular problem for tightly formatted television news). This included historical essays, time lines, news archives, maps, official documents, biographies of protagonists, still photos, video and audio reports, and more. Sites also featured message boards (ABC's quickly accumulated 20,000 postings), chat rooms, and links to other sources. Some news organizations' online services sent their own reporters to the Balkans, where they filed live Web reports.

Other sites were made available by non-news organizations, such as the Federation of American Scientists, which offered current and archived international news stories and press releases, analyses of NATO and Serb military operations, a gallery of propaganda posters, and drawings by Kosovar Albanian children.

The Ministry of Foreign Affairs of the Federal Republic of Yugoslavia site included articles from Yugoslav and (favorable) foreign media, and a section labeled "NATO Aggression." On the other side of the war, the NATO Web site offered official information and video from bombing runs. The United Nations High Commissioner for Refugees provided Web information about the status of Kosovar refugees, and the International Criminal Tribunal for the Former Yugoslavia included records of its war crimes trials. Smaller special-interest organizations and even individuals developed Web sites as forums for their own information and viewpoints.[26] Families could post information about missing relatives, relief agencies could solicit donations, people trapped in the midst of the fighting could send e-mail descriptions of what was happening.

The news consumers perusing such sites take and believe whatever they want. This is unmediated media; there is no editor or network anchor sifting through and selectively presenting this news. Journalists similarly could use the Web to gather information from primary sources. But the public and the journalists faced a common problem: How were they to know what was true? As well as being a valuable medium for news, the Web is a powerful vehicle for propaganda. An e-mail message appears on a relief agency's site, purportedly from a witness to atrocities perpetrated by vengeful Kosovar Albanians. Who *really* sent it, an actual witness or a Serb provocateur?

Appearance on even an established Web site does not necessarily confer legitimacy on such information, any more than a phone call from a person not known by a reporter would be considered valid without being thoroughly checked. Journalists' responsibility is clear— recognize the potential for deception inherent in the accessibility of the Web, and do not rely on Web information without corroborating the identity of the source and the substance of what the source provides. For most reporters, such caution is second nature. News consumers who get their news from the Web should also adopt this standard (and should embrace constructive skepticism generally) as protection against being manipulated.

Not only journalists are interested in checking the authorship of Web dispatches. Governments also may want to know who is sending e-mail and otherwise using the Internet. During the Kosovo War there was particular concern that the Milosevic government might be tracing e-mail it didn't like in order to act against its senders. In response, a California company, Anonymizer.com, began the Kosovo Privacy Project to provide a proxy server as an electronic intermediary through which Yugoslav Web users could visit Web sites and send their messages while keeping them from being traced.[27] This kind of protection further opens the Web news universe to people who fear government retaliation if they search beyond official channels for information. If news organizations encourage online communication, they might consider providing such a shield for those who want to send e-mails, participate in chat rooms, or otherwise use the interactive tools that news Web sites feature.

Given the virtually infinite scope of the Internet and the vast quantity of supplemental online information that news organizations can provide, questions arise about responsibility for the product delivered to the public. Although proprietors of a Web news site may have no problem vouching for their own news stories, most of these sites provide links to additional information. Sometimes the link is to the news organization's own material, such as related stories. But often the link carries a reader to independent sources.

During the Kosovo War, American news organizations' sites provided links to NATO, Yugoslav government agencies, and various interest groups, most of which were intent on promoting their own versions of events, sometimes with more concern about impact than about accuracy. These groups offered still more links.

To what extent is the original news site responsible for linked content? If, for example, CNN provides a link to a pro-Kosovo Liberation Army site, is the network vouching for that site's information? Presumably no; the link is provided as a service to CNN site visitors so they may electronically wander through as much information as they want. But although they may follow a lengthy path of links, they started their journey at CNN, which they trust, and they might assume that CNN's imprimatur is on whatever information they get, even from links. Such naivete will probably dissipate as more people become knowledgeable about the Web, but news organizations should consider providing clear notice to their sites' visitors when they are leaving the premises and entering territory where the information may not meet the original site's standards for accuracy and balance. Some news organizations do this already (CNN notes that "these sites are not endorsed"), but the practice could be more widespread.

The mass of information available online about stories such as the Kosovo War has created a need for the quasi-journalistic information broker who pulls together news, government documents, and other items, then adds sophisticated military and political analysis, and presents all this as a coherent information product. One company doing this is the U.S.-based Stratfor, which claims: "We don't just provide information. We provide intelligence." Writing in *The American Spectator*, Christopher Caldwell called Stratfor "the single most accurate source of news" during the Kosovo War, and said that "the war going on at its Web address looked very different from the war as presented by press-conference-dependent Western newspapers."[28] The product Stratfor offers (most of which is available only to paying subscribers) is closer to an intelligence briefing than a news story. The company's reports often rely on background information that news organizations tend not to use because it cannot be attributed, even though it is probably accurate. When this kind of information package was available in the past, it was usually in a specialized publication, such as a niche magazine or scholarly journal, that could not be as timely as an online product. Journalists as well as sophisticated news consumers will probably begin using such information-gathering services more regularly.

Stratfor found an audience. During the Kosovo War, its daily e-mail newsletter, "Global Intelligence Update," had nearly 40,000 subscribers and its Web site had approximately four million page views each month. Stratfor's reports about NATO bombing patterns drew on e-mails from Yugoslav subscribers who sent word when bombs were dropping.[29] The subscriber as online source will probably become more common.

Other examples of the material available on the Web include the site of the London-based Institute for War and Peace Reporting (iwpr.net), which pulls together news about conflicts around the world for anyone who cares to read it. Crimesofwar.org, the site of the Washington-based Crimes of War Project, publishes an online magazine. Other organizations provide valuable updates about conflict-related issues. Lots of information is becoming available. Whether that will translate into a more knowledgeable public is yet to be determined.

Another online product, the chat room, was popular during the Kosovo War. The chat room has proved to be a useful forum that expands the accessibility of journalists and newsmakers. This is the Web's much-touted interactivity at work, giving members of the public the opportunity to ask their own questions.

This feature can be controversial. Among the guests of MSNBC's chat room was Zeljko Raznatovic, better known as Arkan, indicted for war crimes as the leader of a Serb paramilitary unit renowned for its viciousness. (He also appeared on ABC's *Good Morning, America* and NBC's *Today*.) He received about a thousand e-mail queries. Merrill Brown, editor-in-chief of MSNBC's online division, said the chat room interview was proper because Arkan was "a figure of considerable significance in his country."[30] CNN's Christiane Amanpour, however, said: "He is one of the most brutal psychopathic killers to patrol the Balkans. . . . It simply isn't all right to allow somebody like that unfettered access to the airwaves to sally forth live and unchallenged." She added that people such as Arkan, "indicted for the gravest of crimes against humanity, are not chat-show guests. Just imagine giving Hitler's henchmen a platform just to air their views."[31]

In a standard interview format, the journalist conducting the interview will presumably challenge the person being interviewed, supplying context and pointing out inconsistencies and outright falsehoods. The chat room, however, might provide no interlocutor. So the question for news organizations concerns whether the public will bring adequate knowledge and skepticism to these exchanges. If not, the chat room might be nothing more than a propaganda pulpit. As with other aspects of Web-based news, the use of this kind of unmediated media would benefit from some caution as it develops.

Despite such issues, the Internet proved, even before the Kosovo War, to be a positive influence in the interests of democracy in the former Yugoslavia. In its news and non-news functions, the Web broke through constraints that repressive governments have used to control communication. Radio B92's Veran Matic and Drazen Pantic wrote: "The 1996–97 antigovernment demonstrations became known as the 'Internet Revolution' because of our sophisticated use of the Internet, which allowed students to gather enormous support around the world for their demonstrations and to mobilize anyone interested in a show of solidarity. Internally, in coordination with Radio B92, we used the Internet to alert people to the demonstrations without interference by the state security apparatus," which had cut off regular radio transmission.[32] Those demonstrations were unsuccessful in dislodging the Milosevic regime, but in 2000, when Milosevic finally was toppled by Yugoslavs' votes and outrage, the Internet was one of the tools used to rally his opponents.

Given the value of the Internet in various aspects of the war, it is not surprising that computers have become targets in cyber combat. After NATO began its bombing campaign, Yugoslav hackers sent waves of e-mails—with viruses attached—to NATO headquarters in Brussels. NATO computers had to be taken off-line briefly. Milosevic supporters also hacked into some U.S. government sites, including the White House and Departments of Energy and Interior. The Pentagon reported as many as 100 attempts daily to hack into its computer system.[33] News organizations' Web sites are also susceptible to such intrusions.

As for counterattacks, Ivo Daalder and Michael O'Hanlon report that NATO considered using cyber warfare but limited its efforts to airborne jamming that targeted Serb air defense computers. For U.S. policymakers, there were two reasons for reluctance: American cyber warfare capabilities were still fairly rudimentary, and there were concerns about legal ramifications if attacks on computers caused major damage to the Yugoslavs' civilian infrastructure.[34]

This new dimension of warfare will probably reach maturity in the next conflict, when adversaries have better mastered the strategies and tactics of cyber combat. New kinds of damage—physical and intellectual—will be inflicted. Such are the ways civilization proceeds.

New Tools and Evolving Standards

The ever more sophisticated gadgetry of journalism has made its presence known in small ways as well as large. One of the journalist's most valuable new tools is the cell phone, or, even better, the satellite phone, which is not dependent on local telecommunications systems. For reporting from war zones or other distant places, these telephones have become indispensable. Used with a computer, they can transmit words and pictures, bringing a new dimension to live reporting. During the Kosovo War, some journalists put these phones to another good use, lending them to refugees so they could contact family members elsewhere in the world.

Television and other news media delivered the harrowing story of these refugees into homes throughout the world. Their situation became known as it was developing, not after the fact as had happened in many instances in the past. For much of the public, these fleeing Kosovars were an appropriate casus belli.

This will be a factor in future decisions about intervention. A *Wall Street Journal* editorial said: "In today's world of instant communication, foreign policy cannot succeed without making a place for human rights. We suspect, indeed, that the key foreign policy issue of the new millennium will be defining the role of humanitarianism. Kosovo and before it Bosnia put the issue starkly: Armed gangs invade villages, kill the men, rape the women, burn the houses, and send hordes of refugees fleeing across borders; can the rest of the world stand by and still think of itself as civilized?"[35]

Although the journalist's job remains that of reporting what is happening, the advent of "humanitarian war" may mean more emphasis on covering war crimes, refugees, and other elements of conflict beyond actual combat. This presents some challenges to news judgment. The news audience is assumed to love pathos, and news organizations may indulge their penchant for drama by transforming coverage of humanitarian issues into soap opera that overshadows larger matters. Resisting that will test the resolve of news executives.

Another major topic for media analysis will be *how* wars are fought. Reliance on the "immaculate coercion" of an air war is politically attractive, and some would argue that in Kosovo it was politically necessary, at least in terms of American involvement. President Clinton's national security adviser Sandy Berger said that Congress would not have supported the war, and perhaps would have withdrawn funding, had the president not declared that ground troops would not be used. Berger also said that the NATO consensus would have cracked if there had been the prospect of a land war.[36]

Maybe so. But the other side of the argument is that if the goal of the intervention was to save Kosovar lives and stop the Serbs' ethnic cleansing, then using ground troops and tools such as Apache helicopters might have been the most effective way to wage this war. The immediacy of the Kosovo Albanians' jeopardy and the small unit nature of much of the Serb deployment would seem to have demanded a strong NATO presence on the ground. But the technological glitter and protective cocoon of "virtual war" weaponry captured the imagination of news media and the public, pushing aside other concerns about effectiveness.

During future conflicts, one job for journalists will be to bring more hard-edged realism to the public debate about the adequacy of military commitment, particularly in terms of possible military and civilian casualties. This will be especially important if the public becomes more sensitive to the infliction of "collateral damage," which is the genteel term for civilian casualties. During the Persian Gulf War, press and public generally swallowed the Pentagon's claims about limited harm to noncombatants. Some of these claims were not credible when made and were later found to be untrue.

During the Kosovo conflict, civilian casualties became an issue relatively early, as the one-sided safety of the air war was quickly obvious. The news media did a better job during this war than it had in 1991, raising questions about NATO's approach. NATO's own combat video showed that deadly errors will inevitably be committed by even the most diligent air crews when their missions are conducted at the speeds and altitudes that were prescribed in this war by NATO's generals and their civilian bosses.

NATO personnel remained safe while foreign civilians were endangered and the enemy continued to fight. Michael Ignatieff wrote: "This was the moral calculus of war throughout the ages, but in a television age, it has a political cost: would the public at home continue to stand rising civilian casualties if the bombing was not having any discernible military effect?"[37] That question went unanswered in the Kosovo War because the damage to Yugoslavia's infrastructure became so extensive that even Milosevic's resolve had to give way.

While the war is being fought, the news media's task is to inspire public debate about the cost of safety and the results of risk. If it appears that the "collateral damage" is excessive when compared to the damage done to the enemy's ability to wage war, then policymakers should feel compelled to reevaluate how the war is being conducted.

This is one of the issues that may receive more scrutiny as the breadth and speed of war coverage increase. In his book about the Kosovo War, General Wesley Clark wrote: "The new technologies impacted powerfully at the political levels. The instantaneous flow of news and especially imagery could overwhelm the ability of governments to explain, investigate, coordinate, and confirm. . . . It was clear that the new technologies could put unrelenting heavy pressure on policymakers at all levels from the very beginning of any operation."[38]

Clark's concern is a descendant of a principal lesson of the Vietnam War: news coverage of the horrors of combat can undermine policy that is not well defined and convincingly explained to the public. On the other hand, if government officials meet their political responsibilities and justify the course they choose to pursue, even pervasive real-time news coverage will not obstruct that pursuit.

Although those waging war will always try to use the news media as cheerleaders and transmitters of propaganda, journalists should not let themselves be relegated to this role. It is up to the government to make the case for war and for the way it is being conducted. If elected officials and other policymakers fail to do that adequately, the news media should be sure that the public knows about it.

While the Kosovo War captured the world's attention with its state-of-the-art weaponry and information technology, far bloodier fighting elsewhere was getting much less attention. Also, important new issues related to globalization were maturing without adequate news coverage.

The world and the news business continued to change, and as the next chapter illustrates, journalists' responsibilities were changing as well.

CHAPTER SIX

Watching the World

Global journalism changes as the world changes. Ongoing stories need updating; new and overlooked stories need to be brought to the public's attention.

Wars and other crises will continue to occur, but policies that could affect their outcomes can be reshaped. The debate about intervention proceeds, affected by the globalization that overrides artificial barriers between nations.

As change takes place, the news media have the responsibility to capture the attention of an often disengaged public. Individual journalists have their own duties: to witness and to report, and through their coverage to prod policymakers and the public to pay more attention to what is going on around them. The list of stories that need to be covered grows ever longer.

Endless Wars

Philip Gourevitch, who has written much about Africa's recent troubles, said about one of the continent's latest wars: "Oh, Congo. What a wreck. It hurts to look and listen, and it hurts to turn away."[1]

Africa is not alone in its experience of continuous violence. In some ways the beginning of the new millennium is little different from the start of the last one. War remains rooted in primordial savagery; today's version has simply increased the numbers of victims and, in some cases, upgraded the technology of bloodshed. The journalists who report about this fighting understand the wrenching feeling that Gourevitch cites–the pain of watching people suffer and the pain of doubting that the news stories you have written will do them any good.

Other than surrendering to despair, there is no alternative to going on with the work. To remain with the Congo war as an example, the primary journalistic duty is to alert the public to a crisis that most governments–especially those powerful enough to do something about it– would prefer to ignore (or address covertly). Gourevitch attributes the Congo fighting partly to the lingering upheaval in central Africa produced by the genocide in Rwanda several years earlier. He wrote that "the armies of seven African nations and more than a dozen guerrilla and rebel forces have been fighting there, in a conflict so messy, so broad, and so resistant to any comprehensive resolution that it is sometimes spoken of as Africa's First World War."[2]

An International Rescue Committee survey found that the fighting, displacement, hunger, and disease produced by the war had resulted in the deaths of nearly three million people (of whom just several hundred thousand were killed in actual combat).[3] Beyond the devastation within Congo itself, the war has destabilized an entire region, damaging the security and economy of neighboring countries. The United Nations estimated that overall Congo's war has affected 16 million people. During one week of the fighting, for example, 60,000 refugees fled into Zambia. No country can absorb such an influx on a continuing basis, so life in Zambia becomes a victim of another country's war. As the conflict drags on, children are not being educated, disease is not being fought, food is not being grown. These factors ensure that problems will continue long after the gunfire ends.[4]

When news organizations cover such wars, it is important to examine why nations respond or do not respond to other countries in distress. American policymakers were quite pleased with themselves for fighting a "humanitarian" war in Kosovo, but a moral imbalance exists when the United States ignores far more devastating wars elsewhere. Even without editorializing in favor of interventionism, news coverage should address this inconsistency. Treating wars as isolated episodes and the responses to those wars as similarly isolated political decisions neglects larger issues. Scrutinizing the policymaking process and holding the policymakers accountable are part of journalists' mandate.

Some government officials recognize that new wars demand new policies. Addressing America's role, Richard Holbrooke, who brokered the

Bosnia peace agreement at Dayton in 1995, wrote that in future conflicts, "the world's richest nation, one that presumes to great moral authority, cannot simply make worthy appeals to conscience and call on others to carry the burden."[5] Beyond covering the debate about policy content, the news media also must monitor its implementation. As Holbrooke said about the lack of muscle behind the Dayton Accords, "Good policy badly executed becomes bad policy."[6]

Policy coverage involves analysis of evolving national roles and obligations, which may reflect changing perceptions of sovereignty. An altered, less absolutist definition of sovereignty can affect the legitimacy of intervention. This is a complicated legal and political issue. The UN Charter forbids intervening "in matters which are essentially within the jurisdiction of any State," except when failure to intervene would conflict with the Security Council's duty to preserve peace. Kofi Annan has offered a broad interpretation of the Security Council's right to intervene even in a "domestic" conflict: "In a world where globalization has limited the ability of States to control their economies, regulate their financial policies, and isolate themselves from environmental damage and human migration, the last right of States cannot and must not be the right to enslave, persecute, or torture their own citizens."[7]

Bill Clinton, addressing U.S. troops during the Kosovo War, seemed to adopt Annan's view and endorse a broader approach to interventionism than he had previously supported. "We can say to the people of the world," he proclaimed, "whether you live in Africa, or Central Europe, or any other place, if somebody comes after innocent civilians and tries to kill them en masse because of their race, their ethnic background, or their religion, and it's within our power to stop it, we will stop it."[8]

That is a far more forceful pronouncement than anything said during the Rwanda war five years earlier. Nevertheless, the effect of the president's remarks, and those of the secretary general, is debatable. Although Clinton and Annan's words may indicate a shift in philosophy, there is little evidence of a commensurate shift in policy. President George W. Bush has indicated that he will be extremely cautious when intervention is an option.

Meanwhile, in a less philosophical undertaking, news organizations contemplate changes in the way the world works, such as in the conduct of war between technologically sophisticated states. New wars may not be well suited to traditional news coverage. Instead of reporting about troops on the ground or even presenting video from bomb-mounted cameras, news organizations might be faced with covering cyber warfare in which the most lethal weapons are computer viruses unleashed against an enemy's military (and perhaps civilian) infrastructure.[9] Who is attacking whom may be hard to determine when the combatants are launching their salvos from computers thousands of miles away from their electronic enemy.

This kind of virtual war lends itself to secrecy because it can be conducted in ways that are invisible to press and public. Journalists will be more dependent than ever before on official sources for information. New semantics will also come into play. In addition to air sorties, bomb tonnage, and numbers of killed and wounded, the quantification of war will include numbers of e-mails sent, viruses spread, and computer systems crippled.

But it will still be war and still be devastating. News organizations must be prepared to cover this kind of fighting as well as the conflicts that are still fought with machetes.

In those wars, Congo's experience is likely to be replicated, with the number of actual combat casualties dwarfed by those falling prey to the ripple effects of war. As he considers the future role of the United Nations in armed conflict, Kofi Annan has noted that in the First World War approximately 90 percent of those killed were soldiers. In World War II, civilians (including those killed in the German death camps) constituted slightly more than half of all those killed. In today's conflicts, says Annan, it is common "to put the proportion of civilian casualties somewhere in the region of 75 percent."[10]

Globalization and Its Discontents

Replacing the Cold War's ideological divisions is new stratification based on technology and wealth. Harvard University professor Jeffrey Sachs wrote: "A small part of the globe, accounting for some 15 percent of the earth's population, provides nearly all of the world's technology innovations. A second part, involving perhaps half of the world's population, is able to adopt these technologies in production and consumption. The remaining part, covering around a third of the world's population, is technologically disconnected, neither innovating at home nor adopting foreign technologies."[11]

Prosperity gravitates to the first and smallest of these domains and perpetuates itself. Hunger and disease there are minimal, compared to the rest of the world. When war breaks out in the first or even second of these parts of the world, it almost always involves fewer casualties, as a percentage of population, than occur in conflicts elsewhere. Compare, for instance, the figures from the Balkans to those from central Africa.

The first of these groups of nations is also home to the most influential news media. Their relatively benign environment may foster nearsightedness as these news organizations look at the world. Limited vision works against their responsibility to search for stories that deserve to be brought to the public's attention.

The changes in international political and economic structure increase the challenge to journalists as they watch the world. In his *New York Times* article about Bill Clinton's foreign policy legacy, David Sanger wrote: "In the new world, leaders accustomed to setting their nations' agendas found themselves subject to the judgments of foreign investors. If a country's deficits looked too high, its ability to repay loans too dubious, or if political chaos made it unsafe for new factories, money would move out with the flick of a few keys. Alliances meant little, and traditional foreign aid seemed trivial. Cash flowed to the most competitive countries; those unable to swim in the new sea found life rafts unavailable."[12]

That appraisal of the pronounced shift toward greater interdependence implicitly defines the task for journalists: to recognize the new criteria for exercising power in the world. The economic factors that Sanger mentions will redefine relationships among nations and will reshape the internal characteristics of countries. This will affect the welfare of citizens and the stability of governments. The foreign policy of world powers will change accordingly.

A small but meaningful example can be seen in relations between the United States and Angola. During the Cold War, Angola was viewed by the United States as a Soviet pawn, with a Marxist regime bolstered by Cuban troops. What was then a major concern sounds quaint today. Now Angola finds itself with substantial offshore oil reserves that may provide 10 percent of America's imported oil within a decade or so.[13] This could be the start of a beautiful friendship.

This is how the geopolitical scene changes. It doesn't always happen with the dramatic flourish of the Berlin Wall coming down, but instead takes place in increments that occur at the measured pace of an oil rig boring into the ocean floor.

The tectonic shifts that lie ahead will produce unpredictable effects, defying attempts by governments, news organizations, or others to create a foolproof formula for dealing with change. Building a stronger, up-to-date intellectual foundation for news coverage may be a daunting task, but it is badly needed if the news product is to be appropriately comprehensive. During the Cold War, some journalists–like some policymakers–lapsed into generalizations about "communists," not differentiating between the different goals and tactics of a Stalin, a Tito, and a Ho Chi Minh. Today, comparable misjudgments are being made–again by some journalists and policymakers, among others–about other topics. The results of such sloppiness are uniformly bad.

Coverage of Islam is one example of this. Many news stories about the Middle East and countries elsewhere with large Muslim populations, such as Indonesia and Bosnia, simplistically depict complex political and religious issues, giving news consumers a distorted view of important events. This coverage relies on stereotypes, usually with a pejorative spin. In addition to undermining news accuracy, these stereotypes reinforce biases, nurturing reflexive anti-Muslim sentiment. The Muslim world is multifaceted and Islam is a sophisticated religion, but such matters rarely surface in news stories. For too many news consumers, the word most associated with Islam is "terrorist." The news media are not wholly at fault for this, but they bear considerable responsibility. The principal problem is not journalists' malice or intentional misrepresentation, but rather intellectual laziness. In most cases, that can be cured with a dose of self-discipline.

Plenty of emerging stories demand attention, but no news organization has enough resources to cover them all. Determining what will make up the day's news offerings is one of journalists' most important tasks. The power to *exclude* is particularly significant because it keeps an issue outside the public's field of vision. Web-based news is a partial remedy because it so greatly expands the volume of material that a news organization can provide. But before even a Web site can feature a story, someone has to find it and report it.

Criteria vary when news organizations decide what issues and events merit coverage. Beyond the obvious "must cover" items, such as a presidential address, the decisions are often subjective. Magnitude, in terms of numbers of people affected, is a factor. Competitive pressures are also involved; what other news organizations are doing is always monitored. Editors and producers may also be influenced by lobbying: a politician touting a pet issue, a relief organization urging that attention be paid to a crisis in the making. After these and other matters are taken into account, at the heart of the decision is the definition of "newsworthy"–what the public *needs*, as well as *wants*, to know.

Sometimes the momentum of coverage builds slowly. The continuing spread of AIDS, for example, has only gradually attracted the amount of news coverage it deserves in Western countries. Although treatments such as protease inhibitors have become available to limit the destructiveness of the disease in the most medically advanced nations, elsewhere AIDS keeps spreading explosively, especially in Africa. A study conducted by the U.S. Census Bureau reports that life expectancy in the African countries hardest hit by AIDS will drop to thirty years by 2010.[14] In Zambia, the country's health minister has estimated that half that country's population of approximately 10 million will eventually die of AIDS. The epidemic devastates even those who do not contract the disease, especially the children orphaned when their parents die of AIDS. In Zambia, about half of all the children are malnourished, 20 percent severely so. The U.S. Agency for International Development estimates that largely because of AIDS, nineteen sub-Saharan African countries will have 40 million orphans by 2010.[15]

The response to this must be twofold: renewed efforts to prevent the spread of the disease and to treat those who contract it, and relief programs to help repair the secondary social and economic damage that AIDS does to individuals and communities. To be effective, this must be a massive endeavor, requiring great generosity by the world's richest nations. As a matter of politics, that will happen only if the public in those countries is supportive, and that will depend to some extent on how well informed people are about the issue. Few political leaders can be expected to act decisively on their own initiative about this; the news media will need to be the driving force for meaningful progress.

Coverage of AIDS expanded in 2001 as the mammoth proportions of the crisis became more widely recognized. Coverage should continue to grow in frequency and depth to ensure that the public does not overlook AIDS devastation, even if much of it occurs far away.

The AIDS story leads to a larger issue: Should access to lifesaving medicine be considered a human right, upheld by the community of nations? This involves complex and expensive matters related to pharmaceutical trade and patents, issues that should be explained to the public. By April 2000, this topic was becoming more visible, getting attention from politicians and protestors at the World Bank meeting in Washington.[16] But it is not merely an issue for esoteric political debate. Millions of lives are affected daily. People around the world need to know more about this; the news media need to tell them.

Responding to the AIDS epidemic in Africa, governments and pharmaceutical companies in 2001 expanded their assistance projects. But even these efforts were terribly inadequate, given the scope of the medical disaster. Continued media scrutiny might help push these efforts forward.

The AIDS story is merely one example of the kind of topic that many people might care about if their attention can be drawn to it. Similarly important matters will remain on the fringes of the issues agenda unless news coverage makes them more salient. Environmental topics are among these. For instance, issues related to the availability of water will become increasingly significant. Former Soviet president Mikhail Gorbachev wrote in 2000: "Water, not unlike religion and ideology, has the power to move millions of people. . . . Without water security, social, economic, and national stability are imperiled—a consequence that is magnified where water flows across borders and becomes crucial in regions of religious, territorial, or ethnic tension."[17]

The water-related tensions that Gorbachev cites are part of a larger problem concerning broadly defined environmental issues that much of the world has failed to consider. A 1998 report published by the Carnegie Commission on Preventing Deadly Conflict suggested grim prospects: "The threat of future conflict is firmly located in the developing world—where crowded peoples in poor nations are at risk from the pace of environmental change, the rapid growth in their own populations, the growing threat of infectious disease, and an array of ethnic and tribal hostilities. . . . It is surely possible that at some point one or several 'developing' states might, through their own growth activities, present an environmental threat perceived as so serious that 'developed' states, having pursued other avenues of resolution in vain, decide to intervene militarily to prevent the developing nations from polluting or cutting their forests or exploiting some common-pool resource."[18]

Gloomy scenarios such as that can be fascinating, with some far more credible than others. But these cautionary messages can lead reporters to important, less speculative stories that merit immediate coverage. This is part of defining a properly broad news agenda, which is one of the most challenging tasks facing the news business today.

That job is made more complicated by the changing economics of the news business, specifically the acquisition of news organizations by non-news media corporations. This sometimes jeopardizes traditional journalistic values. Writing in the *Washington Post*, Jim Hoagland cited the business conference in Shanghai at which Sumner Redstone, head of Viacom (which owns CBS), urged journalists to avoid being "unnecessarily offensive" to foreign countries that they cover. Hoagland also noted that Time Warner chief Gerald Levin, trying to curry favor with the Chinese at this meeting, presented Premier Jiang Zemin with a statue of Abraham Lincoln, to whom, wrote Hoagland, "Jiang likes to compare himself for no obvious reason."

On another occasion, James Murdoch—Rupert Murdoch's son, who heads the Asian division of his father's News Corporation—publicly criticized Falun Gong, a religious group banned by the Chinese government. Calling Falun Gong an "apocalyptic cult," Murdoch went on to say that the Western news media had been unfair in their negative portrayals of China.[19]

Executives such as these are strangers to journalism except to see it as another profit center in their diverse enterprises. Their job is to find ways to make more money, in this case by being allowed to tap into the riches of the vast Chinese market. Their actions send a signal to their news employees to respect corporate priorities more than journalistic ones. Hoagland wrote: "The advance of technology demands enormous changes in the information business. It also demands a continuity in values and standards that should not come under even indirect attack from those in positions of leadership."[20]

Hoagland's warning is appropriate, but it is unlikely to have much effect. Just when news organizations should be aggressively expanding the scope of coverage to address important new issues, they are being reined in by corporate bosses who see such efforts as endangering the bottom line. The AIDS in Africa story, for instance, requires a sizable commitment of time and money if it is to be done properly. Important advertisers, such as pharmaceutical companies, may be unhappy about aspects of the coverage. Even if it is reported, there is no telling if the public or policymakers will pay attention.

Given that uncertainty, and if profits are the highest priority, why bother? But if finding and publishing the truth about an important issue— regardless of reaction—is most important, then the story must be told.

The Storytellers' Mandate

One of the challenges facing the global journalist is to avoid being surprised. Dramatic stories often seem to the public to have emerged from nowhere, but that is rarely the case. Famine does not take hold overnight. Wars do not erupt spontaneously. A regional economic meltdown is not a fluke.

These are the kinds of stories that test news organizations' creativity and judgment. How can they be covered as they develop? What kind of reporting will capture the attention of the restless news audience? Some journalists add a corollary to this: How can they be reported in ways that might spur action by policymakers?

The essence of the journalist's job is to tell stories that need to be told. The telling should be accurate, persuasive, and timely. Michael Ignatieff wrote of the need for the news media "to intervene before torture becomes genocide, before racist persecution becomes mass expulsion, and religious conflict becomes civil war. They would have to get to the scene, in other words, before the ambulances arrive."[21]

In terms of doing good, journalism is part of a larger process. People read, hear, or see the news and–at least sometimes–respond. That is where politics comes in, sending the food or tents or money or troops or whatever else might help resolve the problem at hand. Writing during the 2000 presidential campaign, Anthony Lewis said, "Americans do not like to see mass cruelties ignored by the one country that can stop them."[22] That probably is correct, but questions remain about how far Americans or citizens of other powerful nations will go in contributing money and possibly lives to help distant peoples.

News coverage may affect political psychology about such matters, at least to a point. Martin Bell wrote that if "it is possible to create and maintain a climate of opinion in which the saving of lives is thought to matter, and governments are committed to it because their people support it, and survivors in the war zones are given some hope when they would otherwise have none, then something beyond mere hand-wringing is being achieved. And if journalists do it they are committing useful journalism. There is a point to it. It does something other than fill a slot in a schedule."[23]

"Useful journalism" is not redundant. Some of what the news media deliver is mere froth. The reporting that Bell describes is notable for the professional skill that enhances its ability to provoke thinking.

The impact of coverage will vary. Intervention in armed conflict will remain a matter for contentious political debate, no matter how thoroughly the news media report the suffering of innocents. Nonmilitary humanitarian assistance is less politically charged because the costs of providing such aid will usually be measured in money rather than in casualties.

But even when just nonmilitary help is called for, inertia in the policy process can be powerful. News coverage can sometimes loosen its hold. One example in 2000 was the response to the devastating floods in Mozambique. Video of South African Defense Force helicopters rescuing flood victims from trees spurred relief efforts that helped prevent a cholera epidemic and in other ways saved lives. The BBC had moved an antenna dish into the disaster area, which was the key to getting timely television coverage to the rest of the world. UNICEF's Ian McLeod said, "Unless news executives broadcast television images, there won't be public pressure to send help."[24]

Over the years, there have been plenty of examples similar to this one, proving that news coverage can shake awake a dozing public. No one is certain how often this can be done and how long the public will remain awake. Compassion fatigue will take hold at some point. Journalists know this and can respond only by doing their jobs so well that the public's interest will be held as long as possible.

That is a vague prescription, but precision is difficult when trying to calculate the impact of coverage. The moral mandate for the news media concerning such matters is to remain more attentive than the public and the policymakers are, and rely on a broad definition of what news consumers need to know.

The Mozambique case slipped from public attention quickly. It was not the worst catastrophe, and its coverage has been matched or surpassed on many other occasions. It does, nevertheless, illustrate how doing journalism *can* be equated with doing good (a formula that does not apply in every instance). Some journalists may be wary of being cast as social workers, arguing that it is not their job to calculate the effects of their coverage. A declaration of detachment might seem appropriate for a profession that is properly protective of its independence. It also, however, is disingenuous. Why bother doing journalism if it has no effect?

The journalists who cover the unsettling events of post–Cold War turmoil may sometimes need to resist the temptation to step beyond the role of dispassionate observer. Paul Watson, who covered Africa for the *Toronto Star*, wrote: "Soldiers are trained to kill, doctors to save lives. But journalists are supposed to stand and watch so that the rest of the world might see."[25] That separation remains the standard for mainstream news organizations. Serge Schmemann, deputy foreign editor of the *New York Times*, said: "We are not referees in the various conflicts of the world. We are there to report what is happening and let the readers decide whether it is truly horrible or not."[26]

Fair enough. Standing outside the story may be the best way to ensure the objective journalism most likely to win the attention of a public that tends to be skeptical of journalists' motives.

But when journalists do cling to objectivity in the midst of horror, they sometimes are criticized for that, too. The public never makes up its mind about how involved in a story it wants its news gatherers to be.

Kevin Carter learned this. A photographer covering the war in the Sudan in 1993, Carter came upon a little girl, apparently weakened by hunger, sitting in the grass near a relief center. A vulture had settled on the ground nearby.

Carter took the picture. Looking at the photo, it is easy to imagine that the vulture was eyeing the girl as prey. The picture was published throughout the world, and in 1994 it won the Pulitzer Prize for Carter. With attention then focused on him, Carter was asked what he had done after taking the photo. Had he picked up the girl and carried her to the aid station?

He had not. He said that after taking the photograph, he had chased away the vulture, and then he sat down against a tree, smoked a cigarette, and cried. The child continued on her own. Surprised and wounded by the criticism that accompanied his celebrity as a Pulitzer winner, Carter noted that helping one child didn't occur to him when he was in the midst of so many thousands like her. He told a friend, though, that after thinking about it, "I'm really, really sorry I didn't pick the child up."[27]

Carter witnessed so much horror and became so saddened by it. Several months later, he committed suicide.

In her book *Compassion Fatigue*, Brandeis University professor Susan Moeller wrote about this case: "Being close enough to photograph the starving child meant being close enough to help. The responsibility to bear witness does not automatically outweigh the responsibility to be involved."[28] Some might see that as a harsh judgment about Kevin Carter's actions; others might view it as an appropriate moral mandate for journalists who have the opportunity to help a fellow human being.

When addressing individual rather than systemic responses to the world's horrors, critics might keep in mind what the journalists on the ground are going through. They, of course, usually can go home, which spares them the endless hopelessness that refugees and other victims endure. But while doing their stories, they are often subject to many of the same privations and fears as affect the people they cover. And journalists don't always come home. Each year, there are journalists around the world killed while doing their jobs: gunned down by a trigger-happy soldier at a roadblock; turned on by a mob that takes out its fury on the outsider; targeted by a politician who doesn't like being scrutinized by the press.

That is not a plea for sympathy. Journalists know what they are getting into. But it is a suggestion that news consumers and news critics consider how difficult it can be—physically and emotionally—to do journalism.

In 1938, Neville Chamberlain chose to abandon Czechoslovakia to Adolf Hitler rather than intervene in "a quarrel in a far away country between people of whom we know nothing."[29] Today, thanks largely to the news media, no country or people is so far away that we can claim to know nothing about it.

Knowledge increases responsibility. But as post–Cold War political morality takes shape, responsibility to others has yet to be adequately defined. The 2000 American presidential campaign and the outset of George W. Bush's administration were marked by casual distancing from problems that did not directly affect narrowly defined "strategic interests." The United States and other world powers cannot be expected to embrace open-ended interventionism, but the strongest and richest nations do not have the moral right to avert their gaze from injustices that they could halt or at least limit.

The news media must serve as the persistent conscience of the newest world order. That will be no easy task, given the magnitude of evil that emerges from even the limited number of events and issues discussed in this book.

News coverage does not, in itself, determine policy, despite what proponents of "the CNN effect" might contend. But it does wield influence in the democratic interaction between public and government.

That influence is one factor of many in the making of policy. If journalists fail to investigate and report and prod, moral drift will replace moral purpose at a time when scourges of the past might be vanquished.

Today's global journalist confronts a world in which justice and peace remain elusive. That makes more significant the journalist's most important role: to be the witness who arouses conscience.

Notes

Chapter One

1. David Hackett Fischer, *Paul Revere's Ride* (New York: Oxford University Press, 1994), 324–25.

2. James F. Hoge Jr., "Foreign News: Who Gives a Damn?" *Columbia Journalism Review*, November/December 1997, 52.

3. Ian Hargreaves, "Is There a Future for Foreign News," *Historical Journal of Film, Radio, and Television*, vol. 20, no. 1, March 2000, 58.

4. Martin Bell, *In Harm's Way* (London: Penguin, 1996), 127.

5. Warren Christopher, *In the Stream of History* (Stanford: Stanford University Press, 1998), 347.

6. William Shawcross, *Deliver Us from Evil* (New York: Simon and Schuster, 2000), 385.

7. Shawcross, *Deliver Us from Evil*, 122.

8. Michael Ignatieff, *Virtual War* (London: Chatto and Windus, 2000), 204.

9. Shawcross, *Deliver Us from Evil*, 86.

10. Shawcross, *Deliver Us from Evil*, 42.

11. Andrew S. Natsios, *U.S. Foreign Policy and the Four Horsemen of the Apocalypse* (Westport, Conn.: Praeger, 1997), 133–34.

12. Davis Merritt, *Public Journalism and Public Life* (Hillsdale, N.J.: Lawrence Erlbaum Associates, 1995), 116.

13. Ignatieff, *Virtual War*, 179.

14. Bell, *In Harm's Way*, 216.

15. Walter Lippmann, *Public Opinion* (New York: Free Press, 1965), 226.

16. Jonathan Mermin, *Debating War and Peace* (Princeton: Princeton University Press, 1999), 143, 151.

17. Madeleine Albright, remarks at the "Conflicts and War Crimes: Challenges for Coverage" seminar sponsored by the Crimes of War Project and the Freedom Forum, Arlington, Virginia, May 5, 2000, 2, 6.

18. Henry Kissinger, *Does America Need a Foreign Policy?* (New York: Simon and Schuster, 2001), 27.

19. Rick Grant, "Manufacturing Content," *Ottawa Citizen,* April 20, 2000, A15.

20. Philip Gourevitch, *We Wish to Inform You That Tomorrow We Will Be Killed with Our Families* (New York: Picador, 1999), 186.

21. Andrew Natsios, "Illusions of Influence: The CNN Effect in Complex Emergencies," in *From Massacres to Genocide,* edited by Robert I. Rotberg and Thomas G. Weiss (Cambridge, Mass.: World Peace Foundation/Brookings Institution, 1996), 164.

22. Stephen Hess, *International News and Foreign Correspondents* (Washington: Brookings Institution, 1996), 99.

23. John C. Hammock and Joel R. Charny, "Emergency Response as Morality Play: The Media, the Relief Agencies, and the Need for Capacity Building," in *From Massacres to Genocide,* edited by Robert I. Rotberg and Thomas G. Weiss (Cambridge, Mass.: World Peace Foundation/Brookings Institution, 1996), 125–28.

24. Tal Sanit, "The New Unreality," *Columbia Journalism Review,* May/June 1992, 17.

25. Sanit, "The New Unreality," 17.

26. E. R. Shipp, "The World—or Most of It," *Washington Post,* December 5, 1999, B6.

27. Charles L. Overby, "Editors Revisit Foreign News Strategies," *Freedom Forum and Newseum News,* December 1998, 3.

28. Hoge, "Foreign News: Who Gives a Damn?" 49.

29. Michael Janeway, *Republic of Denial* (New Haven: Yale University Press, 1999), 135.

30. Hess, *International News and Foreign Correspondents,* 43.

31. Nicholas Varchaver, "CNN Takes Over the World," *Brill's Content,* June 1999, 106.

32. Edward Seaton, "The Diminishing Use of Foreign News Reporting," speech to the International Press Institute, Moscow, May 26, 1998, 3.

33. Peter Arnett, "Goodbye, World," *American Journalism Review,* November 1998, 60, 57.

34. See also Philip Seib, *Going Live: Getting the News Right in a Real-Time, Online World* (Boulder, Colo.: Rowman & Littlefield, 2001).

Chapter Two

1. Michael Beschloss and Strobe Talbott, *At the Highest Levels* (Boston: Little, Brown, 1993), 132.

2. Beschloss and Talbott, *At the Highest Levels,* 135.

3. Bernard Gwertzman, "Memo to the *Times* Foreign Staff," *Media Studies Journal,* vol. 7, no. 4 (Fall 1993), 38.

4. David Halberstam, "The Powers That Were," *Brill's Content,* September 2000, 26.

5. Steven Livingston, "The New Information Environment and Diplomacy," paper prepared for the International Studies Association meeting, Washington, D.C., February 16–20, 1999, 3.

6. Nik Gowing, "Media Coverage: Help or Hindrance in Conflict Prevention," report to the Carnegie Commission on Preventing Deadly Conflict, September 1997, 6.

7. Stephen Badsey, "The Media and UN 'Peacekeeping' Since the Gulf War," *Journal of Conflict Studies,* vol. XVII, no. 1 (Spring 1997), 19.

8. Ignatieff, *Virtual War,* 187.

9. Clark Clifford, *Counsel to the President* (New York: Random House, 1991), 474.

10. Gowing, "Media Coverage: Help or Hindrance," 12.

11. Quoted in Michael Dobbs, "Foreign Policy by CNN," *Washington Post National Weekly Edition,* July 31, 1995, 24.

12. Christiane Amanpour, "Television's Role in Foreign Policy," *Quill,* April 1996, 16.

13. Rony Brauman, "When Suffering Makes a Good Story," in *Somalia, Rwanda, and Beyond,* edited by Edward R. Girardet (Dublin: *Crosslines Global Report* and the Italian Academy for Advanced Studies at Columbia University, 1995), 137.

14. Gowing, "Media Coverage: Help or Hindrance," 20.

15. Quoted in Shawcross, *Deliver Us from Evil,* 114.

16. Quoted in Ignatieff, *Virtual War,* 20.

17. Henry Kissinger, *Diplomacy* (New York: Simon and Schuster, 1994), 833.

18. Shawcross, *Deliver Us from Evil,* 384.

19. Quoted in Shawcross, *Deliver Us from Evil,* 151.

20. Fareed Zakaria, "Our Hollow Hegemony," *New York Times Magazine,* November 1, 1998, 44.

21. Ignatieff, *Virtual War,* 5.

22. Quoted in Shawcross, *Deliver Us from Evil,* 356.

23. Ignatieff, *Virtual War,* 178.

24. Steven Kull and I. M. Destler, *Misreading the Public* (Washington: Brookings Institution, 1999), 250.

25. Andrew Kohut and Robert C. Toth, "Managing Conflict in the Post–Cold War World: A Public Perspective," paper prepared for the Aspen Institute Conference on Managing Conflict in the Post–Cold War World, Aspen, Colo., August 2–6, 1995, 9.

26. Kull and Destler, *Misreading the Public,* 58.

27. Kohut and Toth, "Managing Conflict," 9.

28. "America's Place in the World II," Pew Research Center for the People and the Press, October 1997, 15.

29. John E. Rielly (ed.), "American Public Opinion and U.S. Foreign Policy 1999," Chicago Council on Foreign Relations, 1999, 4, 12.

30. "America's Place," 27.

31. Rielly, "American Public Opinion," 24–25.

32. Rielly, "American Public Opinion," 26.

33. "America's Place," 29.

34. Kohut and Toth, "Managing Conflict," 14.

35. Peter D. Feaver and Christopher Gelpi, "Shattering a Foreign Policy Myth," *Washington Post National Weekly Edition*, November 15, 1999, 23.

36. Kohut and Toth, "Managing Conflict," 4.

37. Rielly, "American Public Opinion," 6.

38. Kohut and Toth, "Managing Conflict," 18.

39. "Rereading the Public: Isolationism and Internationalism Revisited," *International Studies Perspectives*, vol. 1, no. 2, August 2000, 195–96.

40. Daniel Schorr, "Ten Days that Shook the White House," *Columbia Journalism Review*, July/August 1991, 22.

41. Jack Matlock, "The Diplomat's View of the Press and Foreign Policy," *Media Studies Journal*, Fall 1993, 50.

Chapter Three

1. Peter J. Schraeder, *United States Foreign Policy Toward Africa* (Cambridge, UK: Cambridge University Press, 1994), 177.

2. Susan D. Moeller, *Compassion Fatigue* (New York: Routledge, 1999), 131.

3. Steven Livingston and Todd Eachus, "Humanitarian Crises and U.S. Foreign Policy: Somalia and the CNN Effect Reconsidered," *Political Communication*, vol. 12 (1995), 427.

4. Keith B. Richburg, "Bosnia Pushes Somalia's Brutal War into Shadows," *Chicago Sun-Times*, August 12, 1992, 9.

5. Walter Goodman, "Why It Took TV So Long to Focus on the Somalis," *New York Times*, September 2, 1992, C18.

6. Jonathan Mermin, "Television News and American Intervention in Somalia: The Myth of a Media-Driven Foreign Policy," *Political Science Quarterly*, Fall 1997, 392.

7. Moeller, *Compassion Fatigue*, 153.

8. Don Oberdorfer, "The Path to Intervention," *Washington Post*, December 6, 1992, A1.

9. Smith Hempstone, *Rogue Ambassador* (Sewanee, Tenn.: University of the South Press, 1997), 230.

10. Natsios, *U.S. Foreign Policy and the Four Horsemen of the Apocalypse*, 110.

11. Schraeder, *United States Foreign Policy Toward Africa*, 176.

12. Jonathan Yardley, "In Somalia, a Picture-Perfect Military Maneuver," *Washington Post*, December 14, 1992, B2.

13. Yardley, "In Somalia," B2.

14. Moeller, *Compassion Fatigue*, 145.

15. George F. Kennan, *At a Century's Ending* (New York: Norton, 1996), 295–96.

16. Kennan, *At a Century's Ending*, 297.

17. Kennan, *At a Century's Ending*, 297.

18. Andrew Kohut and Robert C. Toth, "Arms and the People: The Mind of America on Force," *Foreign Affairs*, November/December 1994, 49.

19. William Schneider, "Somalia Sours Public on Intervention," *National Journal*, October 16, 1993, 2512.

20. Jacqueline Sharkey, "When Pictures Drive Foreign Policy," *American Journalism Review*, December 1993, 17.

21. Schneider, "Somalia Sours Public," 2512.

22. Moeller, *Compassion Fatigue*, 146.

23. Colin Powell, *My American Journey* (New York: Random House, 1995), 588.

24. Feaver and Gelpi, "Shattering a Foreign Policy Myth," 22.

25. Robert D. Kaplan, *The Coming Anarchy* (New York: Random House, 2000), 101.

26. Sharkey, "When Pictures Drive Foreign Policy," 18.

27. Scott Peterson, *Me Against My Brother* (New York: Routledge, 2000), 39.

28. Ivo H. Daalder, *Getting to Dayton* (Washington: Brookings Institution Press, 2000), 2.

29. Christopher, *In the Stream of History*, 344.

30. Powell, *My American Journey*, 576.

31. Nik Gowing, "Real-Time TV Coverage from War: Does It Make or Break Government Policy?" in *Bosnia by Television*, edited by James Gow, Richard Paterson, and Alison Preston (London: British Film Institute, 1996), 84.

32. Warren Strobel, "TV Images May Shock but Won't Alter Policy," *Christian Science Monitor*, December 14, 1994, 19.

33. Gowing, "Real-Time TV Coverage from War," 90.

34. Peter Maass, *Love Thy Neighbor* (New York: Knopf, 1996), 76.

35. Maass, *Love Thy Neighbor*, 104.

36. Harry Kreisler, "Witness to Genocide: Conversation with Roy Gutman," Institute of International Studies, University of California at Berkeley, globetrotter.berkeley.edu/conversations/Gutman (accessed October 2000).

37. Bell, *In Harm's Way*, 129.

38. David Rieff, *Slaughterhouse* (New York: Simon and Schuster, 1995), 217.

39. Rieff, *Slaughterhouse*, 216.

40. Sherry Ricchiardi, "Over the Line?" *American Journalism Review*, September 1996, 27.

41. Amanpour, "Television's Role in Foreign Policy," 17.

42. Ricchiardi, "Over the Line?" 27.

43. Eleanor Randolph, "Journalists Find Little Neutrality over Objective Reporting," *Los Angeles Times*, April 22, 1997, A5.

44. Rieff, *Slaughterhouse*, 9.

45. Ricchiardi, "Over the Line?" 25.

46. Michael Dobbs, "How Television Fills the Leadership Vacuum on Bosnia," *Washington Post*, July 23, 1995, C2.

47. Rieff, *Slaughterhouse*, 223.

48. Ricchiardi, "Over the Line?" 27.

49. Randolph, "Journalists Find Little Neutrality," A5.

50. Bell, *In Harm's Way*, 99.

51. Bell, *In Harm's Way*, 114.

52. Tom Shales, "Bosnia's War: ABC News Takes a Stand," *Washington Post*, March 17, 1994, D1.

53. Walter Goodman, "Horror and Despair in the Balkans," *New York Times*, July 25, 1995, C18.

54. Bell, *In Harm's Way*, 108.

55. Roy Gutman, *A Witness to Genocide* (New York: Macmillan, 1993), vii.

56. Gutman, *A Witness to Genocide*, xxxii.

57. Gutman, *A Witness to Genocide*, xli.

58. Sherry Ricchiardi, "Exposing Genocide," *American Journalism Review*, June 1993, 34.

59. M. L. Stein, "A Call for Better International Reporting," *Editor and Publisher*, July 31, 1993, 16.

60. Ricchiardi, "Exposing Genocide," 35.

61. Ricchiardi, "Exposing Genocide," 34.

62. Gowing, "Real-Time TV Coverage from War," 85.

63. Elizabeth Drew, *On the Edge: The Clinton Presidency* (New York: Touchstone, 1995), 411.

64. Nik Gowing, "Real-Time Television Coverage of Armed Conflicts and Diplomatic Crises: Does It Pressure or Distort Foreign Policy Decisions?" Working paper 94-1, Joan Shorenstein Barone Center, John F. Kennedy School of Government, Harvard University, June 1994, 35.

65. R. W. Apple, Jr., "Conflict in the Balkans: Shelling Gives Clinton Chance to Change," *New York Times*, February 8, 1994, A1.

66. Walter Goodman, "Are the TV Images Father to the U.S. Action in Bosnia?" *New York Times*, February 14, 1994, C16.

67. Gowing, "Real-Time Television Coverage of Armed Conflicts and Diplomatic Crises," 28.

68. Michael Elliott, "Why Is the West Scared?" *Newsweek*, February 14, 1994, 24.

69. Laura Silber and Allan Little, *The Death of Yugoslavia* (London: Penguin/BBC, 1995), 298–99.

70. David Rohde, *Endgame* (New York: Farrar, Straus and Giroux, 1997), xv.

71. Rohde, *Endgame*, 350.

72. Charles Lane, "The Fall of Srebrenica," *New Republic*, August 14, 1995, 14.

73. Charles Trueheart, "Journalists Take Aim at Policymakers," *Washington Post*, July 21, 1995, A27.

74. Drew, *On the Edge*, 153.

75. Bob Woodward, *The Choice* (New York: Simon and Schuster, 1996), 262.

76. Rohde, *Endgame*, x.

77. Michael Dobbs and R. Jeffrey Smith, "New Proof Offered of Serb Atrocities," *Washington Post*, October 29, 1995, A1.

78. Randolph, "Journalists Find Little Neutrality," A5.

79. Gowing, "Real-Time Television Coverage of Armed Conflict and Diplomatic Crises," 85.

80. Powell, *My American Journey*, 576.

81. Kohut and Toth, "Managing Conflict," 6.

82. Walter Goodman, "Horror vs. Hindsight: A War of TV Images," *New York Times*, December 4, 1995, C16.

83. Howard Rosenberg, "What We Continue to Miss in Bosnia," *Los Angeles Times*, June 7, 1995, F1.

84. Strobel, "TV Images May Shock," 19.

85. Lord Robertson, "The Work Ahead in Bosnia," *New York Times*, November 25, 2000, A31.

Chapter Four

1. Romeo Dallaire, "The End of Innocence: Rwanda 1994," in *Hard Choices: Moral Dilemmas in Humanitarian Intervention*, edited by Jonathan Moore (Lanham, Md.: Rowman & Littlefield, 1998), 81.

2. Gourevitch, *We Wish to Inform You*, 115.

3. Fergal Keane, "Spiritual Damage," *Guardian*, October 27, 1995, T4.

4. Harry Kreisler, "Reporting the Story of a Genocide: Conversation with Philip Gourevitch," Institute of International Studies, University of California at Berkeley, globetrotter.berkeley.edu/people/Gourevitch/gourevitch-con4.html (accessed November 2000).

5. Thomas Lippman, "Administration Sidesteps Genocide Label in Rwanda," *Washington Post*, June 11, 1994, A1.

6. Moeller, *Compassion Fatigue*, 290.

7. Alain Destexhe, *Rwanda and Genocide in the Twentieth Century* (New York: New York University Press, 1995), 32.

8. Linda Melvern, "Behind Closed Doors," *The World Today*, August/September 2000, 11.

9. Destexhe, *Rwanda and Genocide*, 56.

10. Andrew Natsios, "Illusions of Influence: The CNN Effect in Complex Emergencies," in *From Massacres to Genocide*, edited by Robert I. Rotberg and Thomas G. Weiss (Cambridge, Mass.: World Peace Foundation/Brookings Institution, 1996), 161.

11. Fergal Keane, *Season of Blood* (London: Penguin, 1996), 30.

12. Dallaire, "The End of Innocence," 80.

13. Keane, "Spiritual Damage," T4.

14. James Wooten, "Parachuting into Madness," *Columbia Journalism Review*, November/December 1994, 46.

15. Donatella Lorch, "Genocide Versus Heartstrings," in *Somalia, Rwanda, and Beyond*, edited by Edward R. Girardet (Dublin: *Crossline Global Report* and the Italian Academy for Advanced Studies at Columbia University, 1995), 106.

16. Kreisler, "Reporting the Story of a Genocide," 5.

17. Keane, *Season of Blood*, 108.

18. John Eriksson, "Synthesis Report–The International Response to Conflict and Genocide: Lessons from the Rwanda Experience," Steering Committee of the Joint Evaluation of Emergency Assistance to Rwanda, March 1996, www.reliefweb.int (accessed November 2000).

19. Edith M. Lederer, "Panel Issues Rwanda Genocide Report," *Washington Post*, July 8, 2000, A14.

20. Scott R. Feil, "Preventing Genocide: How the Early Use of Force Might Have Succeeded in Rwanda," Report to the Carnegie Commission on Preventing Deadly Conflict, April 1998, 9.

21. Kofi Annan, "Transcript of Press Conference in Gigiri, Kenya," United Nations press release SG/SM/6547, May 4, 1998.

22. Bill Clinton, "Remarks by the President to Genocide Survivors, Assistance Workers, and U.S. and Rwanda Government Officials," Kigali, Rwanda, March 25, 1998, www.whitehouse.gov/Africa/19980325-16872.html (accessed November 2000).

23. Annan, "Transcript of Press Conference," May 4, 1998.

24. Gourevitch, *We Wish to Inform You*, 297.

25. Gowing, "Media Coverage: Help or Hindrance," 11.

26. Moeller, *Compassion Fatigue*, 275.

27. Elizabeth Kastor, "Indelible Images," *Washington Post*, September 30, 1994, F1.

28. Presidential candidates' debate, October 11, 2000, washingtonpost.com/wp-srv/onpolitics/elections/debatetext101100.htm (accessed November 2000).

29. Natsios, *U.S. Foreign Policy and the Four Horsemen of the Apocalypse*, 32.

30. "Seven Million People Forced to Flee Last Year," U.S. Committee for Refugees news release, June 13, 2000.

31. Blaine Harden, "In Africa, a Lesson in How Not to Keep the Peace," *New York Times*, May 14, 2000, 4-1.

32. Peterson, *Me Against My Brother*, 175.

33. Jim Hoagland, "Africa Abandoned," *Washington Post*, May 11, 2000, A35.

34. Harden, "In Africa, a Lesson," 4-4.

35. Kofi Annan, *The Question of Intervention* (New York: United Nations Department of Public Information, 1999), 13.

36. Michael O'Hanlon, "How to Keep Peace in Africa without Sending Troops," *New York Times*, January 8, 2001, A21.

37. Harden, "In Africa, a Lesson," 4-4.

38. Hoagland, "Africa Abandoned," A35.

39. Jesse Jackson, "War Without the Spotlight," *Chicago Sun-Times*, May 30, 1999, 33.

40. Steve Coll, "The Other War," *Washington Post,* January 9, 2000, W8.

41. Coll, "The Other War," W8.

42. James Traub, "Inventing East Timor," *Foreign Affairs,* July/August 2000, 77.

43. Andy Kershaw, "The Week in Radio," *Independent* (London), September 11, 1999, F8.

44. Maggie O'Kane, "The Only Show in Town," *Guardian,* October 30, 2000, M8.

45. Traub, "Inventing East Timor," 79.

46. Michael Shari, "Petro Trouble," *Business Week,* November 6, 2000, 68E2.

47. Michael J. Smith, "Humanitarian Intervention Revisited," *Harvard International Review,* Fall 2000, 73.

48. Michael J. Smith, "On Humanitarian Intervention," in *Protection Against Genocide,* edited by Neal Riemer (Westport, Conn.: Praeger, 2000), 127.

49. S. Austin Merrill, "Witnesses for the Prosecution," *Columbia Journalism Review,* September/October 1999, 36.

50. Richard Goldstone, "Foreword," in *Crimes of War,* edited by Roy Gutman and David Rieff (New York: W. W. Norton, 1999), 15, 16.

51. Ed Vulliamy, "'Neutrality' and the Absence of Reckoning: A Journalist's Account," *Journal of International Affairs,* Spring 1999, 605.

52. Vulliamy, "'Neutrality' and the Absence of Reckoning," 603.

53. Vulliamy, "'Neutrality' and the Absence of Reckoning," 618.

54. Vjera Bogati, "Courtside: Keraterm Camp Trial–Guardian Witness," Institute for War and Peace Reporting, www.iwpr.net/index.pl?archive/tri/tri_223_4_eng (accessed June 2001).

55. Simon England, "World's Media Loses Interest in Reporting Balkan Horrors," *Dominion* (Wellington, New Zealand), November 3, 1997, 6.

56. Henri Astier, "Rights of the Despised," *American Prospect,* August 14, 2000, 32.

57. Astier, "Rights of the Despised," 31.

58. International Criminal Tribunal for Rwanda, *The Prosecutor v. Jean-Paul Akayesu,* case no. ICTR-96-4-T, section 7.7, paragraph 687. www.ictr.org/ENGLISH/Akayesu/judgement/akay001.htm (accessed November 2000).

59. Marlise Simons, "Three Serbs Convicted in Wartime Rapes," *New York Times,* February 23, 2001, A1.

60. Seth Mydans, "Sexual Violence as Tool of War: Pattern Emerging in East Timor," *New York Times,* March 1, 2001, A1.

61. International Criminal Tribunal for Rwanda, *The Prosecutor v. Georges Ruggiu,* case no. ICTR-97-32-I. www.ictr.org/ENGLISH/cases/Ruggiu/judgement/rug010600.htm (accessed November 2000).

Chapter Five

1. Ivo H. Daalder and Michael E. O'Hanlon, *Winning Ugly: NATO's War to Save Kosovo* (Washington: Brookings Institution Press, 2000), 94.

2. Ignatieff, *Virtual War,* 41.

3. "Erasing History: Ethnic Cleansing in Kosovo," report released by the U.S. Department of State, May 1999.

4. Paul Watson, "Reports Detail Cycle of Violence in Kosovo," *Los Angeles Times,* December 7, 1999, A9.

5. Maggie O'Kane, "We Reported; We Did Not Lie," *Observer,* July 11, 1999, 28.

6. William Safire, "Lessons of Kosovo," *New York Times,* June 7, 1999, A23.

7. O'Kane, "We Reported," 28.

8. Sherry Ricchiardi, "Searching for Truth in the Balkans," *American Journalism Review,* June 1999, 24.

9. Ignatieff, *Virtual War,* 72.

10. Wesley K. Clark, *Waging Modern War* (New York: PublicAffairs, 2001), 442.

11. John-Thor Dahlburg, "Tight-lipped NATO Irks Reporters," *Los Angeles Times,* April 22, 1999, A20.

12. Howard Kurtz, "U.S. Tack: Demonize Enemy, Tightly Control Information," *Washington Post,* March 27, 1999, A13.

13. Calvin Woodward, "NATO Telling Public Little of Raids' Details," *Milwaukee Journal Sentinel,* April 12, 1999, 10.

14. Patrick Sloyan, "The Fog of War," *American Journalism Review,* June 1999, 33.

15. Ignatieff, *Virtual War,* 52.

16. O'Kane, "We Reported," 28.

17. Polly Toynbee and David Walker, *Did Things Get Better?* (London: Penguin, 2001), 129.

18. "Fair Coverage of Kosovo May Not Be 'Balanced,'" *Freedom Forum and Newseum News,* May 1999, 2.

19. Daalder and O'Hanlon, *Winning Ugly,* 111.

20. Paul Watson, "Anatomy of Violence in Kosovo," *Los Angeles Times,* December 22, 1999, A1.

21. "A War-induced Ratings Spike," *American Journalism Review,* June 1999, 39.

22. Ignatieff, *Virtual War,* 139.

23. Carol Guensburg, "Online Access to the War Zone," *American Journalism Review,* May 1999, 12.

24. Veran Matic and Drazen Pantic, "War of Words: When the Bombs Came, Serbia's B92 Hit the Net," *The Nation,* November 29, 1999, 34.

25. Philip M. Taylor, "Propaganda and the Web War," *The World Today,* June 1999, 12.

26. David M. Durant, "Web Watch," *Library Journal,* September 1, 1999, 134.

27. April Lynch, "Kosovo Being Called First Internet War," *San Francisco Chronicle,* April 15, 1999, A12.

28. Christopher Caldwell, "Stratfor.com Is Changing the Way We Think About News," *American Spectator,* September 1999, 42.

29. James Ledbetter, "The Intelligence War Moves Online," *Industry Standard,* June 21, 1999. www.the standard.com (accessed December 2000).

30. J. D. Lasica, "Conveying the War in Human Terms," *American Journalism Review,* June 1999, 76.

31. "Fair Coverage of Kosovo," 2.

32. Matic and Pantic, "War of Words," 34.

33. Rod Nordland, "War: E-Zone Combat," *Newsweek*, October 11, 1999, 72.

34. Daalder and O'Hanlon, *Winning Ugly*, 146.

35. "Why Kosovo?" *Wall Street Journal*, April 16, 1999, A14.

36. Daalder and O'Hanlon, *Winning Ugly*, 97.

37. Ignatieff, *Virtual War*, 62.

38. Clark, *Waging Modern War*, 8.

Chapter Six

1. Philip Gourevitch, "Forsaken," *New Yorker*, September 25, 2000, 65.

2. Gourevitch, "Forsaken," 55.

3. Karl Vick, "An Apocalypse in Congo," *Washington Post National Weekly Edition*, May 7, 2001, 16.

4. "In the Heart of Darkness," *Economist*, December 9, 2000, 27.

5. Richard Holbrooke, *To End a War* (New York: Random House, 1998), 369.

6. Holbrooke, *To End a War*, 337.

7. Annan, *The Question of Intervention*, 33.

8. Bill Clinton, "Remarks by the President to the KFOR Troops," Skopje, Macedonia, June 22, 1999, clinton3.nara.gov/WH/New/Europe-9906/html/Speeches.

9. Ignatieff, *Virtual War*, 196.

10. Annan, *The Question of Intervention*, 5.

11. Jeffrey Sachs, "A New Map of the World," *Economist*, June 24, 2000, 81.

12. David E. Sanger, "Economic Engine for Foreign Policy," *New York Times*, December 28, 2000, A1.

13. "Angola: America's Good New Friend," *Economist*, October 7, 2000, 56.

14. Daniel Q. Haney, "AIDS Could Drop Life Expectancy to 30," *Milwaukee Journal Sentinel*, July 11, 2000, 6A.

15. "Orphans of the Virus," *Economist*, August 14, 1999, 35.

16. Laurie Garrett, *Betrayal of Trust* (New York: Hyperion, 2000), 570.

17. Mikhail Gorbachev, "Out of Water," *Civilization*, October/November 2000, 82.

18. Donald Kennedy, "Environmental Quality and Regional Conflict," report to the Carnegie Commission on Preventing Deadly Conflict, December 1998, 61, 62.

19. Bill Carter, "Murdoch Executive Calls Press Coverage of China Too Harsh," *New York Times*, March 26, 2001, C8.

20. Jim Hoagland, "Disgrace in Shanghai," *Washington Post National Weekly Edition*, October 11, 1999, 5.

21. Michael Ignatieff, *The Warrior's Honor* (New York: Henry Holt, 1997), 32.

22. Anthony Lewis, "Bush in the World," *New York Times*, September 30, 2000, A27.

23. Bell, *In Harm's Way*, 134.

24. Craig Nelson, "Media Credited for Mozambique Flood Aid," *Milwaukee Journal Sentinel*, March 19, 2000, 17A.

25. Paul Watson, "Witness to Africa," *Toronto Star*, January 22, 1995, F1.

26. Sherry Ricchiardi, "Highway to the Danger Zone," *American Journalism Review*, April 2000, 45.

27. Peter Martin, "'I'm Really Sorry I Didn't Pick the Child Up,'" *Mail on Sunday* (London), October 16, 1994, 42.

28. Moeller, *Compassion Fatigue*, 40.

29. Piers Brendon, *The Dark Valley* (New York: Knopf, 2000), 624.

Bibliography

Books

Annan, Kofi A. *The Question of Intervention.* New York: United Nations Department of Public Information, 1999.

Bell, Martin. *In Harm's Way.* London: Penguin, 1996.

Beschloss, Michael, and Strobe Talbott. *At the Highest Levels.* Boston: Little, Brown, 1993.

Burg, Steven L., and Paul S. Shoup. *The War in Bosnia-Herzegovina.* Armonk, N.Y.: M. E. Sharpe, 2000.

Christopher, Warren. *In the Stream of History.* Stanford, Calif.: Stanford University Press, 1998.

Clark, Wesley K. *Waging Modern War.* New York: PublicAffairs, 2001.

Clifford, Clark. *Counsel to the President.* New York: Random House, 1991.

Daalder, Ivo H. *Getting to Dayton.* Washington: Brookings Institution Press, 2000.

Daalder, Ivo H., and Michael E. O'Hanlon. *Winning Ugly: NATO's War to Save Kosovo.* Washington: Brookings Institution Press, 2000.

Destexhe, Alain. *Rwanda and Genocide in the Twentieth Century.* New York: New York University Press, 1995.

Drew, Elizabeth. *On the Edge: The Clinton Presidency.* New York: Touchstone, 1995.

Garrett, Laurie. *Betrayal of Trust.* New York: Hyperion, 2000.

Garton Ash, Timothy. *History of the Present.* New York: Random House, 1999.

Girardet, Edward R., ed. *Somalia, Rwanda, and Beyond. Crosslines* Special Report 1. Dublin: *Crosslines Global Report* and the Italian Academy for Advanced Studies at Columbia University, 1995.

Gourevitch, Philip. *We Wish to Inform You That Tomorrow We Will Be Killed with Our Families.* New York: Picador, 1999.

Gow, James, Richard Paterson, and Alison Preston, eds. *Bosnia by Television*. London: British Film Institute, 1996.

Gutman, Roy. *A Witness to Genocide*. New York: Macmillan, 1993.

Gutman, Roy, and David Rieff, eds. *Crimes of War*. New York: W. W. Norton, 1999.

Haas, Richard N. *Intervention*. Washington: Brookings Institution Press, 1999.

Hempstone, Smith. *Rogue Ambassador*. Sewanee, Tenn.: University of the South Press, 1997.

Hess, Stephen. *International News and Foreign Correspondents*. Washington: Brookings Institution, 1996.

Holbrooke, Richard. *To End a War*. New York: Random House, 1998.

Huntington, Samuel P. *The Clash of Civilizations and the Remaking of World Order*. New York: Simon and Schuster, 1996.

Ignatieff, Michael. *Virtual War*. London: Chatto and Windus, 2000.

———. *The Warrior's Honor*. New York: Henry Holt, 1997.

Janeway, Michael. *Republic of Denial*. New Haven: Yale University Press, 1999.

Kaplan, Robert D. *The Coming Anarchy*. New York: Random House, 2000.

Keane, Fergal. *Season of Blood*. London: Penguin, 1996.

Kennan, George F. *At a Century's Ending*. New York: W.W. Norton, 1996.

Kissinger, Henry. *Diplomacy*. New York: Simon and Schuster, 1994.

———. *Does America Need a Foreign Policy?* New York: Simon and Schuster, 2001.

Kull, Steven, and I. M. Destler. *Misreading the Public*. Washington: Brookings Institution, 1999.

Lippman, Thomas W. *Madeleine Albright and the New American Diplomacy*. Boulder, Colo.: Westview, 2000.

Lippmann, Walter. *Public Opinion*. New York: Free Press, 1965.

Maass, Peter. *Love Thy Neighbor*. New York: Knopf, 1996.

Mermin, Jonathan. *Debating War and Peace*. Princeton: Princeton University Press, 1999.

Merritt, Davis. *Public Journalism and Public Life*. Hillsdale, N.J.: Lawrence Erlbaum Associates, 1995.

Moeller, Susan D. *Compassion Fatigue*. New York: Routledge, 1999.

Moore, Jonathan, ed. *Hard Choices: Moral Dilemmas in Humanitarian Intervention*. Lanham, Md.: Rowman & Littlefield, 1998.

Natsios, Andrew S. *U.S. Foreign Policy and the Four Horsemen of the Apocalypse*. Westport, Conn.: Praeger, 1997.

Peterson, Scott. *Me Against My Brother: At War in Somalia, Sudan, and Rwanda*. New York: Routledge, 2000.

Powell, Colin. *My American Journey*. New York: Random House, 1995.

Rieff, David. *Slaughterhouse*. New York: Simon and Schuster, 1995.

Riemer, Neal, ed. *Protection Against Genocide*. Westport, Conn.: Praeger, 2000.

Rohde, David. *Endgame*. New York: Farrar, Straus and Giroux, 1997.

Rotberg, Robert I., and Thomas G. Weiss, eds. *From Massacres to Genocide*. Cambridge, Mass.: World Peace Foundation/Brookings Institution, 1996.

Schraeder, Peter J. *United States Foreign Policy Toward Africa.* Cambridge, U.K.: Cambridge University Press, 1994.

Seib, Philip. *Going Live: Getting the News Right in a Real-Time, Online World.* Lanham, Md.: Rowman & Littlefield, 2001.

Shawcross, William. *Deliver Us from Evil.* New York: Simon and Schuster, 2000.

Silber, Laura, and Allan Little. *The Death of Yugoslavia.* London: Penguin/BBC, 1995.

Strobel, Warren P. *Late-breaking Foreign Policy.* Washington: United States Institute of Peace, 1997.

Toynbee, Polly, and David Walker. *Did Things Get Better?* London: Penguin, 2001.

Woodward, Bob. *The Choice.* New York: Simon and Schuster, 1996.

Articles, Chapters, Reports, Etc.

Albright, Madeleine. Remarks at the "Conflicts and War Crimes: Challenges for Coverage" seminar sponsored by the Crimes of War Project and the Freedom Forum, Arlington, Virginia, May 5, 2000.

Alter, Jonathan. "When the World Shrugs." *Newsweek,* April 25, 1994, 34.

Amanpour, Christiane. "Television's Role in Foreign Policy." *Quill,* April 1996, 16–17.

"America's Place in the World II." Pew Research Center for the People and the Press, October 1997.

"Angola: America's Good New Friend." *Economist,* October 7, 2000, 56.

Annan, Kofi. "Statement on Receiving the Report of the Independent Inquiry into the Actions of the United Nations During the 1994 Genocide in Rwanda." United Nations press release SG/SM7263, AFR/196, December 16, 1999.

———. "Transcript of Press Conference in Gigiri, Kenya." United Nations press release SG/SM/6547, May 4, 1998.

Apple, R. W., Jr. "Conflict in the Balkans: Shelling Gives Clinton Chance to Change." *New York Times,* February 8, 1994, A1.

Arnett, Peter. "Goodbye, World." *American Journalism Review,* November 1998, 51–67.

Astier, Henri. "Rights of the Despised." *American Prospect,* August 14, 2000, 30.

Badsey, Stephen. "The Media and UN 'Peacekeeping' Since the Gulf War." *Journal of Conflict Studies,* vol. XVII, no. 1 (Spring 1997), 7–27.

Bogati, Vjera. "Courtside: Keraterm Camp Trial–Guardian Witness." Institute for War and Peace Reporting, www.iwpr.net/index.pl?archive/tri/tri_223_4 (accessed June 8, 2001).

Borger, Julian. "CNN Let Army Staff into Newsroom." *The Guardian* (London), April 12, 2000, 17.

Brauman, Rony. "When Suffering Makes a Good Story." Pp. 135–48 in *Somalia, Rwanda, and Beyond,* edited by Edward R. Girardet. Dublin: *Crosslines Global Report* and the Italian Academy for Advanced Studies at Columbia University, 1995.

Caldwell, Christopher. "Stratfor.com Is Changing the Way We Think About News." *American Spectator,* September 1999, 42.

Carter, Bill. "Murdoch Executive Calls Press Coverage of China Too Harsh." *New York Times*, March 26, 2001, C8.

Clinton, Bill. "Remarks by the President to Genocide Survivors, Assistance Workers, and U.S. and Rwanda Government Officials," Kigali, Rwanda, March 25, 1998. www.whitehouse.gov/Africa/19980325-16872.html.

——. "Remarks by the President to the KFOR Troops," Skopje, Macedonia, June 22, 1999. clinton3.nara.gov/WH/New/Europe-9906/html/Speeches.

Coen, Rachel. "After the 'Humanitarian War.'" *Extra!* November/December 1999, 7–8.

Coll, Steve. "The Other War." *Washington Post*, January 9, 2000, W8.

Dahlburg, John-Thor. "Tight-lipped NATO Irks Reporters." *Los Angeles Times*, April 22, 1999, A20.

Dallaire, Romeo. "The End of Innocence: Rwanda 1994." Pp. 71–86 in *Hard Choices: Moral Dilemmas in Humanitarian Intervention*, edited by Jonathan Moore. Lanham, Md.: Rowman & Littlefield, 1998.

Dobbs, Michael. "How Television Fills the Leadership Vacuum on Bosnia." *Washington Post*, July 23, 1995, C2.

Dobbs, Michael, and R. Jeffrey Smith. "New Proof Offered of Serb Atrocities." *Washington Post*, October 29, 1995, A1.

Durant, David M. "Web Watch." *Library Journal*, vol. 124, no. 14 (September 1, 1999), 134.

Elliott, Michael. "Why Is the West Scared?" *Newsweek*, February 14, 1994, 24.

England, Simon. "World's Media Loses Interest in Reporting Balkan Horrors." *Dominion* (Wellington, New Zealand), November 3, 1997, 6.

"Erasing History: Ethnic Cleansing in Kosovo." Report released by the U.S. Department of State, May 1999.

Eriksson, John. "Synthesis Report—The International Response to Conflict and Genocide: Lessons from the Rwanda Experience." Steering Committee of the Joint Evaluation of Emergency Assistance to Rwanda, March 1996. www.reliefweb.int.

"Fair Coverage of Kosovo May Not Be 'Balanced.'" *Freedom Forum and Newseum News*, May 1999, 1–2.

Feaver, Peter D., and Christopher Gelpi. "Shattering a Foreign Policy Myth." *Washington Post National Weekly Edition*, November 15, 1999, 22–23.

Feil, Scott R. "Preventing Genocide: How the Early Use of Force Might Have Succeeded in Rwanda." Report to the Carnegie Commission on Preventing Deadly Conflict, April 1998.

Gassman, Pierre. "TV Without Government: The New World Order?" Pp. 149–58 in *Somalia, Rwanda, and Beyond*, edited by Edward R. Girardet. Dublin: *Crosslines Global Report* and the Italian Academy for Advanced Studies at Columbia University, 1995.

Getlin, Josh. "Public, Pundits Split over Kosovo Story." *Los Angeles Times*, April 16, 1999, A22.

Girardet, Edward R. "Reporting Humanitarianism: Are the New Electronic Media Making a Difference?" Pp. 45–67 in *From Massacres to Genocide*, edited by Robert I.

Rotberg and Thomas G. Weiss. Cambridge, Mass.: World Peace Foundation/Brookings Institution, 1996.

Goodman, Walter. "Are the TV Images Father to the U.S. Action in Bosnia?" *New York Times*, February 14, 1994, C16.

———. "Horror and Despair in the Balkans." *New York Times*, July 25, 1995, C18.

———. "Horror vs. Hindsight: A War of TV Images." *New York Times*, December 4, 1995, C16.

———. "Why It Took TV So Long to Focus on the Somalis." *New York Times*, September 2, 1992, C18.

Gorbachev, Mikhail. "Out of Water." *Civilization*, October/November, 2000, 82–84.

Gourevitch, Philip. "Forsaken." *New Yorker*, September 25, 2000, 53–67.

Gowing, Nik. "Media Coverage: Help or Hindrance in Conflict Prevention." Report to the Carnegie Commission on Preventing Deadly Conflict, September 1997.

———. "Real-time Television Coverage of Armed Conflicts and Diplomatic Crises: Does It Pressure or Distort Foreign Policy Decisions?" Working paper 94-1, Joan Shorenstein Barone Center, John F. Kennedy School of Government, Harvard University, June 1994.

———. "Real-time TV Coverage from War: Does It Make or Break Government Policy?" Pp. 81–91 in *Bosnia by Television*, edited by James Gow, Richard Paterson, and Alison Preston. London: British Film Institute, 1996.

Grant, Rick. "Manufacturing Content." *Ottawa Citizen*, April 20, 2000, A15.

Guensburg, Carol. "Online Access to the War Zone." *American Journalism Review*, May 1999, 12–13.

Gwertzman, Bernard. "Memo to the *Times* Foreign Staff." *Media Studies Journal*, Fall 1993, 33–40.

Halberstam, David. "The Powers That Were." *Brill's Content*, September 2000, 23–26.

Hammock, John C., and Joel R. Charny. "Emergency Response as Morality Play: The Media, the Relief Agencies, and the Need for Capacity Building." Pp. 115–35 in *From Massacres to Genocide*, edited by Robert I. Rotberg and Thomas G. Weiss. Cambridge, Mass.: World Peace Foundation/Brookings Institution, 1996.

Haney, Daniel Q. "AIDS Could Drop Life Expectancy to 30." *Milwaukee Journal Sentinel*, July 11, 2000, 6A.

Harden, Blaine. "In Africa, a Lesson in How Not to Keep the Peace." *New York Times*, May 14, 2000, 4-1.

Hargreaves, Ian. "Is There a Future for Foreign News?" *Historical Journal of Film, Radio, and Television*, vol. 20, no. 1, March 2000, 55–61.

Hoagland, Jim. "Africa Abandoned." *Washington Post*, May 11, 2000, A35.

———. "Disgrace in Shanghai." *Washington Post National Weekly Edition*, October 11, 1999, 5.

Hoge, James F., Jr. "Foreign News: Who Gives a Damn?" *Columbia Journalism Review*, November/December 1997, 48–52.

Huff, Richard. "Big Three Nets Devote More Time to Colorado Massacre Than Kosovo." *Daily News* (New York), May 7, 1999, 138.

Ignatieff, Michael. "The Next President's Duty to Intervene." *New York Times,* February 13, 2000, WK17.

"In the Heart of Darkness." *Economist,* December 9, 2000, 27–29.

Jackson, Jesse. "War Without the Spotlight." *Chicago Sun-Times,* May 30, 1999, 33.

Kastor, Elizabeth. "Indelible Images." *Washington Post,* September 30, 1994, F1.

Keane, Fergal. "Spiritual Damage." *Guardian,* October 27, 1995, T4.

Kelly, Michael. "Clinton's Empty Words on Killing in Rwanda." *Milwaukee Journal Sentinel,* January 18, 2000, A10.

Kennedy, Donald. "Environmental Quality and Regional Conflict." Report to the Carnegie Commission on Preventing Deadly Conflict, December 1998.

Kershaw, Andy. "The Week in Radio." *Independent* (London), September 11, 1999, F8.

Kohut, Andrew, and Robert C. Toth. "Arms and the People: The Mind of America on Force." *Foreign Affairs,* November/December 1994, 47–62.

———. "Managing Conflict in the Post–Cold War World: A Public Perspective." Paper prepared for the Aspen Institute Conference on Managing Conflict in the Post–Cold War World, Aspen, Colo., August 2–6, 1995.

Kreisler, Harry. "Reporting the Story of a Genocide: Conversation with Philip Gourevitch." Institute of International Studies, University of California at Berkeley. globetrotter.berkeley.edu/people/Gourevitch (accessed October 2000).

———. "Witness to Genocide: Conversation with Roy Gutman." Institute of International Studies, University of California at Berkeley. globetrotter.berkeley. edu/conversations/Gutman (accessed October 2000).

Kurtz, Howard. "Bosnia Overload: Is the Public Tuning Out?" *Washington Post,* September 13, 1993, D1.

———. "U.S. Tack: Demonize Enemy, Tightly Control Information." *Washington Post,* March 27, 1999, A13.

Lane, Charles. "The Fall of Srebrenica." *New Republic,* August 14, 1995, 14.

Lasica, J. D. "Conveying the War in Human Terms." *American Journalism Review,* June 1999, 76.

Ledbetter, James. "The Intelligence War Moves Online." *Industry Standard,* June 21, 1999, www.thestandard.com (accessed December 2000).

Lederer, Edith M. "Panel Issues Rwanda Genocide Report." *Washington Post,* July 8, 2000, A14.

Lewis, Anthony. "Bush in the World." *New York Times,* September 30, 2000, A27.

Lindsay, James M. "The New Apathy." *Foreign Affairs,* September/October 2000, 2–8.

Lippman, Thomas. "Administration Sidesteps Genocide Label in Rwanda." *Washington Post,* June 11, 1994, A1.

Livingston, Steven. "The New Information Environment and Diplomacy." Paper prepared for the International Studies Association Meeting, Washington, D.C., February 16–20, 1999.

Livingston, Steven, and Todd Eachus. "Humanitarian Crises and U.S. Foreign Policy: Somalia and the CNN Effect Reconsidered." *Political Communication*, vol. 12 (1995), 413–29.

Lorch, Donatella. "Genocide Versus Heartstrings." Pp. 99–107 in *Somalia, Rwanda, and Beyond*, edited by Edward R. Girardet. Dublin: *Crossline Global Report* and the Italian Academy for Advanced Studies at Columbia University, 1995.

Lynch, April. "Kosovo Being Called First Internet War." *San Francisco Chronicle*, April 15, 1999, A12.

Maren, Michael. "The Food-Aid Racket." *Harper's*, August 1993, 10–12.

Martin, Peter. "'I'm Really Sorry I Didn't Pick the Child Up.'" *Mail on Sunday* (London), October 16, 1994, 40, 42.

Matic, Veran, and Drazen Pantic. "War of Words: When the Bombs Came, Serbia's B92 Hit the Net." *The Nation*, November 29, 1999, 34–36.

Matlock, Jack. "The Diplomat's View of the Press and Foreign Policy." *Media Studies Journal*, Fall 1993, 49–57.

Mayer, Jane. "Bad News." *The New Yorker*, August 14, 2000, 30–36.

Melvern, Linda. "Behind Closed Doors." *The World Today*, August/September 2000, 9–11.

Mermin, Jonathan. "Television News and American Intervention in Somalia: The Myth of a Media-Driven Foreign Policy." *Political Science Quarterly*, Fall 1997, 385–403.

Merrill, S. Austin. "Witnesses for the Prosecution." *Columbia Journalism Review*, September/October 1999, 35–37.

Morin, Richard. "The World Around Us." *Washington Post National Weekly Edition*, December 25, 2000, 37.

Mydans, Seth. "Sexual Violence as Tool of War: Pattern Emerging in East Timor." *New York Times*, March 1, 2001, A1.

Natsios, Andrew. "Illusions of Influence: The CNN Effect in Complex Emergencies." Pp. 149–68 in *From Massacres to Genocide*, edited by Robert I. Rotberg and Thomas G. Weiss. Cambridge, Mass.: World Peace Foundation/Brookings Institution, 1996.

Nelson, Craig. "Media Credited for Mozambique Flood Aid." *Milwaukee Journal Sentinel*, March 19, 2000, 17A.

Nordland, Rod. "War: E-Zone Combat." *Newsweek*, October 11, 1999, 72.

Oberdorfer, Don. "The Path to Intervention," *Washington Post*, December 6, 1992, A1.

O'Hanlon, Michael. "How to Keep Peace in Africa Without Sending Troops." *New York Times*, January 8, 2001, A21.

O'Kane, Maggie. "The Only Show in Town." *Guardian*, October 30, 2000, M8.

⸻. "We Reported; We Did Not Lie." *Observer*, July 11, 1999, 28.

"Orphans of the Virus." *Economist*, August 14, 1999, 35.

Overby, Charles. "Editors Revisit Foreign News Strategies." *Freedom Forum and Newseum News*, December 1998, 3.

Randolph, Eleanor. "Journalists Find Little Neutrality over Objective Reporting." *Los Angeles Times*, April 22, 1997, A5.

"Rereading the Public: Isolationism and Internationalism Revisited." *International Studies Perspectives*, vol. 1, no. 2 (August 2000), 195–205.

Ricchiardi, Sherry. "Exposing Genocide . . . for What?" *American Journalism Review*, June 1993, 32–36.

———. "Highway to the Danger Zone." *American Journalism Review*, April 2000, 42–49.

———. "Over the Line?" *American Journalism Review*, September 1996, 25–30.

———. "Searching for Truth in the Balkans." *American Journalism Review*, June 1999, 22–28.

Richburg, Keith B. "Bosnia Pushes Somalia's Brutal War into Shadows." *Chicago Sun-Times*, August 12, 1992, 9.

Rielly, John E., ed. "American Public Opinion and U.S. Foreign Policy 1999." Chicago Council on Foreign Relations, 1999.

Robertson, Lord. "The Work Ahead in Bosnia." *New York Times*, November 25, 2000, A31.

Rosenberg, Howard. "What We Continue to Miss in Bosnia." *Los Angeles Times*, June 7, 1995, F1.

Sachs, Jeffrey. "A New Map of the World." *Economist*, June 24, 2000, 81–83.

Safire, William. "Lessons of Kosovo." *New York Times*, June 7, 1999, A23.

Sanger, David E. "Economic Engine for Foreign Policy." *New York Times*, December 28, 2000, A1.

Sanit, Tal. "The New Unreality." *Columbia Journalism Review*, May/June 1992, 17.

Schneider, William. "Somalia Sours Public on Intervention." *National Journal*, October 16, 1993, 2512.

Schorr, Daniel. "Ten Days That Shook the White House." *Columbia Journalism Review*, July/August 1991, 21–23.

Seaton, Edward. "The Diminishing Use of Foreign News Reporting." Speech to the International Press Institute, Moscow, May 26, 1998.

"Seven Million People Forced to Flee Last Year." U.S. Committee for Refugees, news release, June 13, 2000.

Shales, Tom. "Bosnia's War: ABC News Takes a Stand." *Washington Post*, March 17, 1994, D1.

Shari, Michael. "Petro Trouble." *Business Week*, November 6, 2000, 68E2-4.

Sharkey, Jacqueline. "When Pictures Drive Foreign Policy," *American Journalism Review*, December 1993, 14–19.

Shipp, E. R. "The World–or Most of It." *Washington Post*, December 5, 1999, B6.

Simons, Marlise. "Three Serbs Convicted in Wartime Rapes." *New York Times*, February 23, 2001, A1.

Sloyan, Patrick J. "The Fog of War." *American Journalism Review*, June 1999, 32–34.

Smith, Michael J. "Humanitarian Intervention Revisited." *Harvard International Review*, Fall 2000, 72–76.

———. "On Humanitarian Intervention." Pp. 123–39 in *Protection Against Genocide*, edited by Neal Riemer. Westport, Conn.: Praeger, 2000.

Stein, M. L. "A Call for Better International Reporting." *Editor and Publisher*, July 31, 1993, 16.

Strobel, Warren. "TV Images May Shock but Won't Alter Policy." *Christian Science Monitor*, December 14, 1994, 19.

Taylor, Philip M. "Propaganda and the Web War." *The World Today*, June 1999, 10–12.

Traub, James. "Inventing East Timor." *Foreign Affairs*, July/August 2000, 74–89.

Trueheart, Charles. "Journalists Take Aim at Policymakers." *Washington Post*, July 21, 1995, A27.

Varchaver, Nicholas. "CNN Takes Over the World." *Brill's Content*, June 1999, 102.

Vick, Karl. "An Apocalypse in Congo." *Washington Post National Weekly Edition*, May 7, 2001, 16–17.

Vulliamy, Ed. "'Neutrality' and the Absence of Reckoning: A Journalist's Account." *Journal of International Affairs*, vol. 52, no. 2 (Spring 1999), 603–20.

"A War-induced Ratings Spike." *American Journalism Review*, June 1999, 39.

Watson, Paul. "Anatomy of Violence in Kosovo." *Los Angeles Times*, December 22, 1999, A1.

——. "Reports Detail Cycle of Violence in Kosovo." *Los Angeles Times*, December 7, 1999, A9.

——. "Witness to Africa." *Toronto Star*, January 22, 1995, F1.

"Why Kosovo?" *Wall Street Journal*, April 16, 1999, A14.

Woodward, Calvin. "NATO Telling Public Little of Raids' Details." *Milwaukee Journal Sentinel*, April 12, 1999, 10.

Wooten, James. "Parachuting into Madness." *Columbia Journalism Review*, November/December 1994, 46–47.

Yardley, Jonathan. "In Somalia, a Picture-Perfect Military Maneuver." *Washington Post*, December 14, 1992, B2.

Zakaria, Fareed. "Our Hollow Hegemony." *New York Times Magazine*, November 1, 1998, 44–47, 74, 80.

Index

About the Author

Philip Seib is the Lucius W. Nieman Professor of Journalism at Marquette University. He is the author of twelve books, including *Going Live: Getting the News Right in a Real-Time, Online World* and *Headline Diplomacy: How News Coverage Affects Foreign Policy*. He is also a veteran television and newspaper journalist.